Practicing Persuasive Written and Oral Advocacy

Case File III

Practicing Persuasive Written and Oral Advocacy

Case File III

David W. Miller
Professor of Law
University of the Pacific
McGeorge School of Law

Michael Vitiello
Professor of Law
University of the Pacific
McGeorge School of Law

Michael R. Fontham
Adjunct Professor of Law
Tulane University Law School
Partner, Stone, Pigman, Walther, Wittmann & Hutchinson

ΛSPEN

PUBLISHERS

111 Eighth Avenue, New York, NY 10011
www.aspenpublishers.com

© 2005 Aspen Publishers, Inc.
A Wolters Kluwer Company
www.aspenpublishers.com

Aspen Publishers
Attn: Permissions Department
111 Eighth Avenue, 7th floor
New York, NY 10011-5201

Printed in the United States of America.

1 2 3 4 5 6 7 8 9 0

ISBN 0-7355-5664-4

ISSN 1539-4603

About Aspen Publishers

Aspen Publishers, headquartered in New York City, is a leading information provider for attorneys, business professionals, and law students. Written by preeminent authorities, our products consist of analytical and practical information covering both U.S. and international topics. We publish in the full range of formats, including updated manuals, books, periodicals, CDs, and online products.

Our proprietary content is complemented by 2,500 legal databases, containing over 11 million documents, available through our Loislaw division. Aspen Publishers also offers a wide range of topical legal and business databases linked to Loislaw's primary material. Our mission is to provide accurate, timely, and authoritative content in easily accessible formats, supported by unmatched customer care.

To order any Aspen Publishers title, go to *www.aspenpublishers.com* or call 1-800-638-8437.

To reinstate your manual update service, call 1-800-638-8437.

For more information on Loislaw products, go to *www.loislaw.com* or call 1-800-364-2512.

For Customer Care issues, e-mail *CustomerCare@aspenpublishers.com*; call 1-800-234-1660; or fax 1-800-901-9075.

Aspen Publishers
A Wolters Kluwer Company

CONTENTS

CONTENTS

INTRODUCTION

THE CASE FILE: *PETRILLO V. ROOKS*

Case File III brings a new lawsuit to the series, *Practicing Persuasive Written and Oral Advocacy*.[1] The case of *Ernestine Petrillo v. Linwood Rooks, Harriett Yun, and Bald Mountain Community Church*, raises issues of tort and agency law, federal and state constitutional law as to the relationship of church and state, application of the testimonial privilege pertaining to members of the clergy, and federal subject matter jurisdiction based on diversity of citizenship.

The issues in *Petrillo v. Rooks* are raised by means of various procedures under the Federal Rules of Civil Procedure. These include motions to dismiss pursuant to Rule 12(b)(1) and (6), a motion to compel discovery pursuant to Rule 37(a)(2), a motion for summary judgment pursuant to Rule 56, and an appeal from a final judgment of a U.S. district court to a U.S. court of appeals. In addition to the pleadings and motions, *Case File III* contains several depositions, which provide evidentiary foundation for the substantive issues.

Case File III is a rich instructional tool for use in such law school courses as Civil Procedure, Pre-Trial Practice, Appellate Advocacy, Persuasive Writing and both Basic and Advanced Legal Research and Writing. The materials on which *Case File III* is based were developed, used, and refined for two years in the Appellate Advocacy course at the University of the Pacific McGeorge School of Law. Based on that experience, we are confident that you—law professors and law students alike—will find *Case File III* to be an excellent instructional resource.[2]

THE STORY

In addition to its instructional merits, *Case File III* tells an interesting and rather poignant story. Here is a summary of the story.

Ernestine Petrillo, a kindergarten teacher, was a troubled young woman with a lot of money. She was devastated when her parents died in an auto accident and five months later her fiancé broke off their engagement. She sought help from the Pastoral Counseling Center at her church, Bald Mountain Community Church ("BMCC") in Bald Mountain, Alabama.

Rev. Linwood Rooks was a gifted and popular pastoral counselor. He was called to be director of the Pastoral Counseling Center and an Associate Pastor at BMCC less than a year before Ms. Petrillo became his client. Over several months in counseling, he helped Ms. Petrillo emerge from the shell of grief and self-doubt in which she was trapped. He encouraged her to improve her image and act

---

[1] *Case Files I* and *II* are both based on *Coburn v. Martinez*, in which a psychiatrist sought injunctive relief to prevent a journalist from publishing tape recordings of confidential sessions with a client. The client was a police officer who had fatally shot an unarmed prisoner attempting to escape. *Case File I* raises issues of service of process and personal jurisdiction over the operator of a Web site. *Case File II* deals with freedom of speech and of the press under the First Amendment and also raises a novel issue of vicarious liability for an intentional tort. They are both available from Aspen Publishers. *Case File I* is ISBN 0-7355-2452-1, and *Case File II* is ISBN 0-7355-3644-9.

[2] We have used our own textbook to accompany the case files and supplement lectures. Michael R. Fontham, Michael Vitiello, and David W. Miller, *Persuasive Written & Oral Advocacy in Trial & Appellate Courts* (Aspen Law & Business 2002, ISBN 0-7355-2450-5).

with greater confidence. He also suggested that she be more aggressive in investing the inheritance from her late parents.

Unknown to Ms. Petrillo, Rev. Rooks had a serious conflict of interest. A business that he and a partner operated was about to go broke. It desperately needed cash. Rooks persuaded Ms. Petrillo to invest $132,000 in this business without disclosing that it was nearly insolvent.

The business, R&B, a limited partnership, was formed to carry out an ambitious plan hatched by Rev. Rooks and his friend, Rev. Heather Sedalia Burr. R&B was to acquire and operate a chain of bed and breakfast inns with a religious program that would attract vacationers seeking both recreation and spiritual uplift. The inns would be staffed by clergy people who would lead the religious programs and serve as genial hosts.

R&B raised enough capital and debt financing to purchase, renovate, and begin operating two inns. But the enterprise lost money from the beginning. It was on its last legs when Rev. Rooks persuaded Ms. Petrillo to invest in it.

Soon R&B was bankrupt, Ms. Petrillo's $132,000 was gone, and Rooks was charged with criminal violations of state securities law.

Ms. Petrillo's lawyer discovered that Rooks had been admonished in his prior job for soliciting investments from counseling clients. The lawyer also discovered evidence that BMCC's Senior Pastor, Rev. Harriett Yun, was aware of Rooks' shady conduct at BMCC.

Rev. Yun is an enterprising religious leader who founded BMCC 25 years ago and built it into a church with 3,000 members and a magnificent building. She is proud of her church's doctrinal liberality and freedom

from hierarchy. While disappointed that Rev. Rooks did not work out as the director of the Counseling Center, she rejected the claim that either she or BMCC should cover Ms. Petrillo's loss.

Ms. Petrillo sued BMCC and Rev. Yun for the losses she suffered on account of her misplaced trust in Rev. Rooks.[3] BMCC and Rev. Yun defended on the grounds that neither of them should be held vicariously liable for Rev. Rooks' misconduct, and they denied that they had been personally negligent in hiring and supervising Rev. Rooks. In addition, they contended that adjudicating the claims against them and granting Ms. Petrillo any secular judicial relief would violate the free exercise and establishment clauses of the U.S. Constitution as well as the Alabama Religious Freedom Amendment.

Before the court could reach the merits of this controversy, it faced a challenge to its jurisdiction. The challenge arose from the fact that soon after the collapse of R&B, Ms. Petrillo moved to Wisconsin to live with her sister and enter a graduate program in library science. When she sued BMCC and Rev. Yun in federal court, she based jurisdiction on diversity of citizenship. BMCC and Rev. Yun, who are both Alabama citizens, contended that Ms. Petrillo remained a citizen of Alabama even after moving to Wisconsin, and thus the federal court did not have diversity jurisdiction.

During discovery, when Ms. Petrillo's lawyer tried to find out what Rev. Yun had been told about Rev. Rooks' pastoral counseling practice, Rev. Yun refused to answer questions in order to protect the

---

[3]Rev. Rooks also was named as a defendant, but he defaulted and appears to be insolvent.

privilege bestowed by Alabama law upon confidential communications to members of the clergy. She claimed this privilege even though the parishioner who had confided in her later decided that she did not need the communication to be kept secret. Ms. Petrillo's lawyer filed a motion asking the court to require Rev. Yun to answer the questions she had refused to answer.

Several other witnesses gave depositions covering Ms. Petrillo's relationship with Rev. Rooks, the history and operations of R&B, and the process by which BMCC had selected and assigned Rev. Rooks to lead the Pastoral Counseling center. When the parties finished discovery, the lawyers for BMCC and Rev. Yun asserted that there was no genuine issue as to any material fact and moved for summary judgment. They argued that their clients were entitled as a matter of law to have Ms. Petrillo's action dismissed on the merits.

DISTRICT COURT'S RULINGS

The district court ruled on the various motions and wrote an opinion to accompany a final judgment, which readied the case for appeal. The court's rulings and opinions are not included in this volume. Rather, alternative versions of them are included in the *Teacher's Manual* for use at the instructor's discretion.

USES OF THIS CASE FILE

Case File III is ideally suited to be used as the record in Moot Court programs or as the centerpiece of a Pre-Trial and Appellate Advocacy course featuring several assignments to brief and argue motions as well as a multi-issue appeal. It is also suitable as source of simulated exercises in a variety of other law school courses, as noted above.

The *Teacher's Manual* guides the instructor in creating assignments of varying degrees of difficulty and complexity, includes research files for assignments that do not have a research component, and contains a memorandum of law to guide judges and graders as to the substantive issues in the case.

SOME CHOICES THE AUTHORS MADE

Petrillo v. Rooks is set in a federal district court because federal rules of practice are accessible to most American law students. A full record is developed in the district court so that students can learn to argue both legal and factual issues, pore over the record to identify those issues, find evidentiary support for their positions, and deal realistically with the challenges of standard of review and harmless error.

The case culminates in a U.S. court of appeals rather than in the U.S. Supreme Court because a court of appeals more accurately simulates the typical appellate practice of most American litigators. In a court of appeals, the issues are more likely to be down-to-earth, and the doctrine of precedent is more robust.

Case File III consists entirely of simulated legal documents. They are simulated because actual litigation papers seldom can achieve precise teaching objectives without being modified for educational purposes. That the documents are simulated does not mean they are unrealistic. In fact, the documents in *Case File III* are exactingly similar in both content and form to documents generated in real litigation.

Case File III contains no notes, comments, or other aids. Real litigation lacks those amenities. The instructor must decide what types of assistance students should receive. The *Teacher's Manual* includes suggestions.

To avoid chronological obsolescence, all dates are relative. "YR-00" refers to the year when you commence using the book, "YR-01" means one year earlier, and "YR+01" means one year in the future. Thus, if you begin using the book in 2006, "YR-02" will stand for 2004. It may be helpful to make a cheat sheet to translate relative years into more familiar numbers.

The case file does not specify days of the week because the events in the case file can take place in any year. For this reason, there should be no room to argue that described events could not have occurred on the date indicated (*e.g.*, that papers are not usually filed in court on Sundays).

ACKNOWLEDGEMENTS

The materials on which *Case File III* is based were first used in Appellate Advocacy courses taught at Pacific/McGeorge by our colleagues Brian Landsberg, George Harris, and Mary-Beth Moylan. We are grateful for their helpful suggestions. In addition, George Harris and Mary-Beth Moylan performed the research and drafting needed to create the issues and documents pertaining to diversity of citizenship and the Alabama Religious Freedom Amendment. We very much appreciate their good work.

The research underlying *Case File III* was supported by grants from the University of the Pacific, McGeorge School of Law. We are grateful for this assistance, as well as for the encouragement we received from Dean Elizabeth Rindskopf Parker and Associate Dean John G. Sprankling.

ERRORS

We have made every effort to achieve accuracy, consistency, and coherence in *Case File III*. If you notice any errors or anomalies, please let us know. Professor Miller is the managing agent for such matters. His telephone number is (916) 739-7006. His e-mail address is *dmiller@pacific.edu.*

We hope you enjoy working with *Case File III*.

D.W.M.
M.V.
M.R.F.

Armand DuPriest
Wilson & DuPriest
900 Maple Lane
Bald Mountain, Alabama 36918
Telephone: (934) 444-2541

In the
United States District Court
for the Western District of Alabama

Ernestine Petrillo,	)	
	)	
Plaintiff	)	Civil Action No. 00-85FD
	)	
v.	)	
	)	
Linwood Rooks,	)	
Harriett Yun, and	)	
Bald Mountain Community Church,	)	
	)	
Defendants	)	

COMPLAINT FOR DAMAGES FOR BREACH OF FIDUCIARY DUTY, FRAUD, VIOLATION OF ALABAMA SECURITIES ACT, AND NEGLIGENCE

1. This is a complaint for damages by Ernestine Petrillo ("Ms. Petrillo"), a former member of Bald Mountain Community Church ("BMCC") in Bald Mountain, Alabama, against Rev. Linwood Rooks ("Rev. Rooks"), the former Associate Pastor of Bald Mountain Community Church, who was Ms. Petrillo's pastoral counselor. Ms. Petrillo seeks damages for Rev. Rooks' breach of fiduciary duty in inveigling Ms. Petrillo to invest in Rev. Rooks' personal business venture, R&B, LP ("R&B"). In addition, she seeks damages from Rev. Rooks for fraud and violation of the Alabama Securities Act in

fraudulently inducing Ms. Petrillo to purchase limited partnership interests in R&B, a failing business venture. Ms. Petrillo also seeks damages against BMCC and its Senior Pastor, Rev. Harriett Yun ("Yun"), who are vicariously liable for the wrongdoing of Rev. Rooks and primarily liable for breaching their duty of care to Ms. Petrillo by their negligence in hiring and supervising of Rev. Rooks.

Jurisdiction (Diversity of Citizenship)

2. The plaintiff, Ms. Petrillo, is a citizen of Wisconsin. The defendants, Revs. Rooks and Yun, are citizens of Alabama. The defendant BMCC is an unincorporated religious association organized under the laws of Alabama with its principal place of business in Bald Mountain, Alabama, and thus is a citizen of Alabama. The amount in controversy exceeds $75,000, exclusive of interest and costs. Therefore, this court has subject matter jurisdiction on the basis of diversity of citizenship pursuant to 28 U.S.C. § 1332(a).

Common Allegations

3. All of the common allegations in paragraphs 4 through 16, below, are incorporated by reference in each of the Counts that follow.

4. Rev. Yun is the Senior Pastor of BMCC, a position she has held since YR-24. As Senior Pastor, she is answerable only to the Church Council, which is the highest governing body of BMCC. Her responsibilities include shepherding the religious and spiritual life of the congregation and promoting the welfare of the community. She is

charged by the Church Council with managing the day-to-day affairs of BMCC. Her

responsibilities include supervising both the ministerial staff, which comprises four

Associate Pastors and a Minister of Music, and the lay staff. In all of the conduct alleged

in this Complaint, Rev. Yun was acting on behalf of BMCC within the scope of her

agency and employment as Senior Pastor.

5.   Ms. Petrillo was a member of BMCC from childhood through June YR-01, when

she left Bald Mountain to settle in Wisconsin, where she is pursuing graduate studies.

Between December YR-03 and May YR-02, Ms. Petrillo suffered two major life

tragedies: her parents died and her engagement to marry was terminated. As a result of

these and other stresses, she believed herself to be in need of pastoral counseling.

6.   Rev. Rooks is an ordained minister and a certified pastoral counselor. He was

called to be Associate Pastor of BMCC and Director of BMCC's Pastoral Counseling

Center in May YR-03 and continued to serve in that capacity until he resigned effective

July 1, YR-01.

7.   Ms. Petrillo was in pastoral counseling with Rev. Rooks from May 18, YR-02,

to April 20, YR-01. Ms. Petrillo sought pastoral counseling from Rev. Rooks on the

recommendation of Rev. Yun, who assured Ms. Petrillo that Rev. Rooks was a competent

and ethical pastoral counselor. Ms. Petrillo also relied on Rev. Rooks' representation that

he was a competent and ethical pastoral counselor.

8.   While in pastoral counseling, Ms. Petrillo developed great trust for Rev. Rooks. She admired Rev. Rooks and wanted to please him. Rev. Rooks actively encouraged Ms. Petrillo's feelings of trust and admiration and encouraged Ms. Petrillo to subordinate her own beliefs and attitudes to those of Rev. Rooks and submissively to accept Rev. Rooks as a wise and benevolent counselor. He asserted himself as a dominating father figure in her life.

9.   During the course of pastoral counseling, Rev. Rooks urged Ms. Petrillo to become more adventuresome in order to confront issues of low self-esteem and timidity. Specifically, Rev. Rooks urged Ms. Petrillo to become more daring in investing the "nest egg" she had inherited from her parents, a sum of about a quarter million dollars.

10.   During the course of pastoral counseling, Rev. Rooks informed Ms. Petrillo about R&B, a limited partnership. He described R&B as a religiously oriented company whose business was to own and operate a small chain of bed and breakfast inns featuring religious decor, a spiritual atmosphere, and hosts who were ordained ministers. He falsely represented that R&B would be a good investment for her in that it would be only slightly risky from a financial perspective, with great upside potential. He encouraged Ms. Petrillo to invest in R&B as a way to confront her chronic timidity, wisely invest her inheritance, and address her profound feelings of alienation from God by becoming involved with a religiously oriented enterprise. He represented that he was personally acquainted with the

founders of R&B and could personally recommend them as pious and prudent entrepreneurs to whom she could entrust her money with confidence.

11. In response to Rev. Rooks' active encouragement, in October YR-02 Ms. Petrillo invested $4,000 in a limited partnership interest in R&B; and in December YR-02 she invested $128,000 in additional limited partnership interests in R&B, an investment that Rev. Rooks told her would be the best possible Christmas present she could give herself.

12. At no time did Rev. Rooks disclose to Ms. Petrillo that he was, in fact, one of the two general partners in R&B. Rev. Rooks and Rev. Heather Sedalia Burr founded R&B in YR-05 and raised capital by marketing limited partnership interests.

13. By early YR-04, R&B had raised sufficient capital to begin buying properties to be operated as religiously oriented bed and breakfast inns. R&B commenced operations in January YR-03 with bed and breakfast properties in Florida and Michigan. The inns were never profitable. In fact, by the end of January YR-02, R&B showed huge operating losses. By January YR-01, R&B stopped paying most of its current bills. Rev. Rooks never informed Ms. Petrillo of any of the foregoing facts. On the contrary, he described R&B as financially sound. In March YR-01, one of R&B's creditors filed an involuntary petition in bankruptcy against R&B, and R&B ceased operations.

14. R&B was already insolvent by the time Rev. Rooks began urging Ms. Petrillo to invest in it, and Ms. Petrillo is informed and believes that none of her investment ever made it into the capital account of R&B but was used directly to pay employees' wages

and for other immediate cash needs. Rev. Rooks disclosed none of these facts to Ms. Petrillo.

15. As a proximate result of the foregoing actions by Rev. Rooks, Ms. Petrillo lost the entire $132,000 that she invested in R&B. She is informed by the trustee in bankruptcy and therefore believes that there will be no assets available to repay anything to the limited partners.

16. As a proximate result of the foregoing actions by Rev. Rooks, Ms. Petrillo suffered great emotional distress, including anger, fear, humiliation, and an overwhelming sense of betrayal and loss. Her anxiety has been so great that she has been unable to work or maintain her home. At great expense, she moved to Wisconsin to be cared for by her sister.

COUNT ONE: Breach of Fiduciary Duty (Rooks)

17. As her pastoral counselor, Rev. Rooks owed Ms. Petrillo a fiduciary duty of loyalty. He breached that duty by allowing and encouraging Ms. Petrillo to invest in an enterprise in which he had a financial interest without full disclosure of his interest, thereby creating a conflict of interest between his own financial well-being and his duty of undivided loyalty to Ms. Petrillo. He breached that duty by lying to Ms. Petrillo about his true motives for encouraging her to invest in L&P. He breached that duty by making false statements about the financial soundness of L&P. Because of Rev. Rooks' dominant role in the relationship, Ms. Petrillo was unable to protect her own interests and relied on the trust she placed in Rev. Rooks. Ms. Petrillo's loss of $132,000 plus her pain

and suffering were the proximate result of Rev. Rooks' breach of fiduciary duty of loyalty to Ms. Petrillo.

COUNT TWO: Fraud (Rooks)

18. As more fully set forth in paragraphs 10-14, above, Rev. Rooks made false representations to Ms. Petrillo concerning the ownership, financial soundness, and financial prospects of R&B, all of which were existing facts that were material to Ms. Petrillo's decision to invest in R&B. Rev. Rooks knew that these representations were false when made, and he made them willfuly with the intent to deceive. In the alternative, Rev. Rooks made these representations recklessly and without regard to their truth or falsity. Ms. Petrillo invested $132,000 in R&B in reliance on Rev. Rooks' false and fraudulent representations.

19. As more fully set forth in paragraphs 10-14, above, Rev. Rooks suppressed numerous material facts concerning R&B, which Rev. Rooks was under an obligation to communicate because of the confidential relationship between Ms. Petrillo and Rev. Rooks.

20. Rev. Rooks consciously and deliberately engaged in the acts of fraud herein alleged.

21. Ms. Petrillo is entitled to recover both compensatory damages to reimburse her loss of $132,000 and punitive damages to punish Rev. Rooks for his fraudulent, wanton, and malicious misconduct.

COUNT THREE: Violation of Alabama Securities Act (Rooks)

22. Partnership interests in R&B were "securities" within the meaning of the Alabama Securities Act. In connection with R&B's sale of limited partnership interests to Ms. Petrillo, Rev. Rooks made untrue statements of material facts and omitted to state material facts necessary in order to make his statements not misleading in the light of the circumstances under which they were made, all as set forth in paragraphs 10-14, above.

23. On or about May 12, YR-01, Ms. Petrillo tendered back to Rev. Rooks, in his capacity as a general partner of R&B, all the limited partnership interests that she had purchased in R&B. This tender was refused.

24. Pursuant to the Alabama Securities Act, Rev. Rooks is liable to Ms. Petrillo for $132,000, the full consideration paid for her limited partnership interests in R&B, together with interest at six percent per year from the dates of payment, court costs, and reasonable attorneys' fees, the amounts of which are as yet unknown to Ms. Petrillo.

COUNT FOUR Respondeat Superior (BMCC and Yun)

25. At all relevant times, Rev. Rooks was employed by either BMCC or Rev. Yun as an Associate Pastor and Director of BMCC's Pastoral Counseling Center. His employment was by mutual consent between himself and BMCC or Rev. Yun, was performed for the benefit of BMCC or Rev. Yun, and was subject to overall supervision and control by Rev. Yun acting on her own behalf or on behalf of BMCC. In all of the conduct alleged

above, Rev. Rooks was acting within the scope of his employment by BMCC or Rev. Yun.

26. Based on the facts alleged in paragraph 25, above, BMCC or Rev. Yun is liable to Ms. Petrillo for all of the damages she suffered as a result of the tortious conduct of Rev. Rooks.

COUNT FIVE: Negligent Hiring (BMCC and Yun)

27. In the evaluation and hiring of persons to serve as Associate Pastor of BMCC and Director of BMCC's Pastoral Counseling Center, BMCC and Rev. Yun had a duty to use reasonable care to hire only persons who were qualified, competent, and ethical. This duty was owed to all of the members of BMCC and to all present and future clients of BMCC's Pastoral Counseling Center, including Ms. Petrillo.

28. If BMCC and Rev. Yun had made reasonable inquiries, they would have discovered that Rev. Rooks' employment history included instances in which he was disloyal to pastoral counseling clients and tried to involve clients in his personal business ventures.

29. BMCC and Rev. Yun failed to make reasonable inquiries into the background and work experience of Rev. Rooks prior to hiring him.

30. Ms. Petrillo suffered the losses alleged herein as a proximate result of the negligence of BMCC and Rev. Yun in hiring Rev. Rooks.

COUNT SIX: Negligent Supervision (Yun & BMCC)

31. As the employer and supervisor, respectively, of Rev. Rooks in his capacity as an Associate Pastor of BMCC and Director of BMCC's Pastoral Counseling Center, BMCC and Rev. Yun had a duty to use reasonable care in supervising Rev. Rooks' conduct in those capacities to insure the safety and well-being of all members of BMCC and all clients in pastoral counseling.

32. BMCC and Rev. Yun knew or should have known that Rev. Rooks was engaging in inappropriate and unethical conduct as a pastoral counselor, in that he was attempting to involve his clients in his personal business ventures. BMCC and Rev. Yun negligently failed to supervise Rev. Rooks to prevent this misconduct.

33. Ms. Petrillo suffered the losses alleged herein as a proximate result of the negligence of BMCC and Rev. Yun in failing adequately to supervise Rev. Rooks.

PRAYER FOR RELIEF

WHEREFORE, Ms. Petrillo, prays for a judgment—

A. Awarding her compensatory damages in the amount of $132,000 for the loss of her investment in L&P;

B. Awarding her prejudgment interest at the rate of six percent per annum on the amount of $132,000 from the time of her purchases of limited partnership interests in L&P until the date of judgment;

C. Awarding her compensatory damages in the amount of $100,000 for the pain and suffering she endured as a result of the defendants' actions;

D. Awarding her punitive damages in the amount of $1,000,000 to punish and make an example of the defendants for their wanton and malicious misconduct;

E. Awarding her costs of suit and reasonable attorneys' fees in amounts to be determined by the court; and

F. Such other and further relief to which she may be entitled.

Dated: January 7, YR-00

Respectfully submitted,

Armand DuPriest

Armand DuPriest

Wilson & DuPriest
900 Maple Lane
Bald Mountain, Alabama 36918
Telephone: (934) 444-2541

Attorney for Plaintiff, Ernestine Petrillo

IN THE
UNITED STATES DISTRICT COURT
FOR THE WESTERN DISTRICT OF ALABAMA

Ernestine Petrillo,	)	
Plaintiff	)	Civil Action No. 00-85FD
v.	)	
	)	
Linwood Rooks, et al.	)	
Defendants	)	

> UNITED STATES DISTRICT COURT
> **FILED**
> **January 11, YR-00**
> WESTERN DISTRICT OF ALABAMA

WAIVER OF SERVICE OF SUMMONS

TO: Armand DuPriest
       Wilson & DuPriest
       900 Maple Lane
       Bald Mountain, Alabama 36918
       Telephone: (934) 444-2541

On behalf of myself, individually, and on behalf of Bald Mountain Community Church, of which I am Senior Pastor and by whom I am authorized to accept service of process, I acknowledge receipt of your request that we waive service of a summons in the above-captioned action. I have also received a copy of the complaint in the action, two copies of this instrument, and a means by which I can return the signed waiver to you without cost to me.

We agree to save the cost of service of a summons and an additional copy of the complaint in this lawsuit by not requiring that we be served with judicial process in the manner provided by Rule 4 of the Federal Rules of Civil Procedure.

We will retain all defenses or objections to the lawsuit or to the jurisdiction or venue of the court except for objections based on a defect in the summons or in the service of the summons.

We understand that a judgment may be entered against us, or either of us, if an answer or motion under Rule 12 is not served upon you within 60 days after January 8, YR-00.

Dated: January 10, YR-00

Harriett Yun
_____
Rev. Harriett Yun
Senior Pastor
Bald Mountain Community Church
200 North Boundary Street
Bald Mountain, Alabama 36819

Emily Rumsdale
Miller, Eldridge & Pasternak
13304 Bald Mountain Parkway
Bald Mountain, Alabama 36918
Telephone (934) 485-9000

UNITED STATES DISTRICT COURT
FILED
January 23, YR-00
WESTERN DISTRICT OF ALABAMA

Attorney for Defendants
Rev. Harriett Yun and
Bald Mountain Community Church

In the
United States District Court
for the Western District of Alabama

Ernestine Petrillo,	)	
	)	
Plaintiff	)	
v.	)	Civil Action No. 00-85FD
	)	
Linwood Rooks, et al.	)	
	)	
Defendants	)	

MOTION TO DISMISS

The defendants Rev. Harriett Yun and Bald Mountain Community Church move pursuant to Fed. R. Civ. P. 12(b)(1) to dismiss the Complaint on the grounds that this Court lacks subject matter jurisdiction over this action and, in the alternative, pursuant to Fed. R. Civ. P. 12(b)(6), to dismiss Counts Four, Five, and Six of the Complaint on the grounds that none of those counts states a claim upon which relief can be granted.

[Document page 1]

LACK OF SUBJECT MATTER JURISDICTION

The Complaint raises no claims under federal law. It alleges jurisdiction solely on the basis of diversity of citizenship under 28 U.S.C. § 1332(b). The diversity required by the statute is, however, lacking.

As alleged in the Complaint, all defendants are citizens of Alabama. Plaintiff alleges that she is a citizen of Wisconsin. However, plaintiff is in fact a citizen of Alabama. She resided in Alabama all of her life until June of YR-01, when she moved to Wisconsin to pursue graduate studies. Since she has no intention to remain indefinitely in Wisconsin, her domicile remains Alabama for purposes of diversity jurisdiction.

For the foregoing reasons, diversity of citizenship is lacking, and the complaint should be dismissed pursuant to Fed. R. Civ. P. 12(b)(1) for lack of subject matter jurisdiction.

FAILURE TO STATE A CLAIM UPON WHICH RELIEF CAN BE GRANTED

Even if this court had subject matter jurisdiction, the complaint should be dismissed for failure to state a claim upon which relief can be granted against the moving defendants, the Rev. Harriett Yun (hereinafter "Rev. Yun") and Bald Mountain Community Church (hereinafter "BMCC").

[Document page 2]

Counts One through Three of the Complaint allege claims for relief only against the defendant Linwood Rooks. The only counts purporting to assert claims against Rev. Yun and BMCC are Counts Four through Six.

<u>Count Four</u>

Count Four alleges that the defendants Yun and BMCC are liable for the conduct of Rev. Rooks described in Counts One through Three on the basis of respondeat superior. Counts One through Three allege that Rev. Rooks duped the plaintiff into investing in a limited partnership in breach of his duty of loyalty as a pastoral counselor and in such a manner as to constitute actionable fraud. Count Four alleges that the events alleged in Counts One through Three took place while Rev. Rooks was purporting to act in the capacity of an Associate Pastor and Pastoral Counselor employed by the defendant BMCC or by the defendant Rev. Yun.

As a matter of law, a pastoral counselor acts outside the scope of his or her employment when he or she endeavors to sell investment securities to a client. Similarly, a pastoral counselor acts outside the scope of his or her employment when he or she swindles a client.

Therefore, the doctrine of respondeat superior does not apply and Count Four should be dismissed.

Counts Five and Six

Counts Five and Six allege that BMCC and Rev. Yun are liable to the plaintiff for damages resulting from the Defendant Rooks' misconduct because they negligently hired and negligently supervised Rooks in his work as a pastoral counselor.

The qualifications of an ordained member of the clergy to be called and ultimately hired as a pastor or associate pastor of a particular church are inextricably bound up with the religious beliefs of the clergy person and the religious needs of the church. The qualifications for an ordained minister to be hired as a pastoral counselor (as opposed to a secular psychotherapist) by a particular church are also tied to the particular counselor's religious viewpoint and philosophy, including most notably the counselor's opinion as to the relative importance in pastoral counseling of Holy Scriptures and the teachings of secular psychologists and allied professionals.

Similarly, the criteria by which a Church Council or a Senior Pastor should supervise a member of the ministerial staff who is serving as a pastoral counselor are inseparable from religious issues and concerns.

This court cannot hear and determine the allegations of Counts Five and Six without becoming entangled in matters of religion, which entanglement would violate both the Free Exercise and the Establishment Clauses of the First Amendment to the United States Constitution.

[Document page 4]

*   *   *   *   *

For the foregoing reasons, as more fully set forth in the accompanying Memorandum of Points and Authorities, the Court should dismiss this action because it lacks subject matter jurisdiction or, in the alternative, should dismiss counts Four through Six of the Complaint for failure to state claims upon which relief can be granted.

Respectfully submitted,

Emily Rumsdale
_____

Emily Rumsdale
Miller, Eldridge & Pasternak
13304 Bald Mountain Parkway
Bald Mountain, Alabama 36918
Telephone: (934) 485-9000

Attorney for the defendants,
Rev. Harriett Yun and
Bald Mountain Community Church

Dated: January 23, YR-00

CERTIFICATE OF SERVICE

I certify that on this 23rd day of January YR-00, I served the foregoing Motion to Dismiss upon the plaintiff, Ernestine Petrillo, by causing a copy thereof to be mailed, first-class postage prepaid, to her attorney of record, Armand DuPriest, Esquire, Wilson & DuPriest, 900 Maple Lane, Bald Mountain, Alabama 36918.

Emily Rumsdale
_____

Emily Rumsdale

Miller, Eldridge & Pasternak
13304 Bald Mountain Parkway
Bald Mountain, Alabama 36918

Attorney for Defendants
Rev. Harriett Yun and
Bald Mountain Community Church

In the
United States District Court
for the Western District of Alabama

Ernestine Petrillo,   )
)
           Plaintiff   )   Civil Action No. 00-85FD
    v.   )

UNITED STATES DISTRICT COURT
FILED
January 29, YR-00
WESTERN DISTRICT OF ALABAMA

Linwood Rooks, et al.   )

Defendants   )

SCHEDULING ORDER

THIS CASE was called for a conference pursuant to Fed. R. Civ. P. 16(b) on this 29th day of January, YR-00.

1. <u>Appearance for the plaintiff</u>. The following counsel appeared for the plaintiff:

> Armand DuPriest
> Wilson & DuPriest
> 900 Maple Lane
> Bald Mountain, Alabama 36918

2. <u>Appearance for the defendants</u>. The following counsel appeared for the defendants Rev. Harriett Yun ("Yun") and Bald Mountain Community Church ("BMCC"):

> Emily Rumsdale
> Miller, Eldridge & Pasternak
> 13304 Bald Mountain Parkway
> Bald Mountain, Alabama 36918

The defendant Rev. Linwood Rooks appeared <u>pro se</u> and informed the court that he will not contest this action and has no interest or desire to participate in any proceedings in this action. The court advised Rev. Rooks of his rights and determined on the basis of further discussion with Rev. Rooks that he has made his choice voluntarily and with full knowledge and understanding of the consequences of failing to appear and defend. In accordance with his wishes, Rev. Rooks was then excused, and the conference proceeded without him.

3. Initial disclosures. Both counsel informed the court and agreed that they have already exchanged the information and made the disclosures required by Fed. R. Civ. P. 26(a), and the court is satisfied that no further orders pursuant to Rule 26(a) are needed at this time.

4. Motion to Dismiss. The defendants Yun and BMCC have filed a motion to dismiss for lack of subject matter jurisdiction (Fed. R. Civ. P. 12(b)(1)) and failure to state a claim upon which relief can be granted (Fed. R. Civ. P. 12(b)(6)). The defendants shall have until February 26, YR-00, to conduct limited discovery confined to the issue of subject matter jurisdiction. The court will hear the motion as to subject matter jurisdiction as soon thereafter as the calendar will allow.

5. Further Proceedings on Motion to Dismiss. If the motion to dismiss for lack of subject matter jurisdiction is denied, then the court will turn to the 12(b)(6) motion. The defendants shall serve their memorandum supporting that motion within seven days after the entry of an order upholding subject matter jurisdiction, and the plaintiff shall serve her response within five days thereafter. The defendants' 12(b)(6) motion will be placed on the calendar for argument as soon thereafter as practicable.

[Document page 2]

6. <u>Initial Depositions</u>.   In the event the motion to dismiss for lack of subject matter jurisdiction is denied, the defendant Yun and the plaintiff have agreed to make themselves available for early depositions. Counsel shall cooperate in arranging for these depositions to be taken promptly but not before the hearing on the defendants' 12(b)(6) motion.

7. <u>Further discovery</u>.   All other discovery is stayed until after those two depositions have been taken.   Thereafter, the parties may notice additional depositions and engage in other discovery, subject to further order of the court. Counsel shall confer and agree upon a convenient schedule for such additional depositions and other discovery. All discovery shall be completed by August 1, YR-00.

IT IS SO ORDERED.

Dated: January 29, YR-00

Francis Drafter
Francis Drafter
United States District Judge

WE CONSENT TO THE ENTRY OF THE FOREGOING ORDER:

Armand DuPriest

Armand DuPriest
Wilson & DuPriest
900 Maple Lane
Bald Mountain, Alabama 36918

Attorney for the plaintiff,
Ernestine Petrillo

Emily Rumsdale

Emily Rumsdale
Miller, Eldridge & Pasternak
13304 Bald Mountain Parkway
Bald Mountain, Alabama 36918
(934) 485-9000

Attorney for Defendants
Rev. Harriett Yun and
Bald Mountain Community Church

[Document page 3]

Armand DuPriest
Wilson & DuPriest
900 Maple Lane
Bald Mountain, Alabama 36918
Telephone: (934) 444-2541

In the
United States District Court
for the Western District of Alabama

Ernestine Petrillo,	)	
	)	
Plaintiff	)	Civil Action No. 00–85FD
v.	)	
	)	
Linwood Rooks,	)	
Harriett Yun, and	)	
Bald Mountain Community Church,	)	
	)	
Defendants	)	

PLAINTIFF'S ANSWERS TO DEFENDANTS' INTERROGATORIES

Interrogatory No. 1: State every place you have resided from the date of your birth until the present.

Answer: From May of YR-25 until September of YR-07, I resided in Bald Mountain, Alabama. From September of YR-07 through June of YR-03, I resided during the school year in Birmingham, Alabama, while attending the University of Alabama at Birmingham, and resided in Bald Mountain, Alabama, during summer vacations. From June of YR-03 until June of YR-01, I resided in Bald Mountain, Alabama, where I taught elementary school. In June of YR-01, I moved to Madison, Wisconsin, where I reside at the present.

[Document page 1]

Interrogatory No. 2: State all reasons for your change of residence to Wisconsin.

Answer: In September of YR-01, I began a masters degree program in library science at the University of Wisconsin in Madison, Wisconsin. I have an older sister who lives in Madison, with whom I now share an apartment. I felt the need to leave Bald Mountain, Alabama because I was traumatized by my relationship with Reverend Rooks and his betrayal of my trust. For the same reason, I was unable to continue my employment as an elementary school teacher in Bald Mountain.

Interrogatory No. 3: State the location of any bank accounts or trust accounts that you maintain or that are maintained for your benefit.

Answer: I have a checking account at First Bank in Madison, Wisconsin. I have a savings account at Alabama Federal Savings and Loan in Bald Mountain, Alabama. A trust account established for my benefit by my parents is maintained at Alabama Federal Savings and Loan in Bald Mountain, Alabama and administered by a trustee affiliated with the savings and loan.

Interrogatory No. 4: In what state, if any, have you been registered to vote at all times from your 18th birthday to the present?

Answer: I was first registered to vote in September of YR-05 in Alabama. In August of YR-01, I registered to vote in Wisconsin.

Interrogatory No. 5: List the location of any votes that you have cast in national, state or local elections from your 18th birthday until the present.

Answer: I voted in Alabama in November of YR-04 and November of YR-02. I have not yet voted in Wisconsin but intend to in November of YR-00.

Interrogatory No. 6: Identify the location(s) of any real property that you own in whole or in part.

Answer: I have a one-fourth joint tenancy interest, together with my three siblings, in a house in Bald Mountain, Alabama, which I inherited from my parents. I have a leasehold interest in an apartment in Madison, Wisconsin, which I hold jointly with my sister Mary Petrillo. The lease will expire in June of YR+01 but is subject to renewal.

Interrogatory No. 7: Describe any and all trips that you have made to Alabama since moving to Wisconsin, including the duration of each visit, where you stayed while in Alabama and the purpose of the visit.

Answer: Between June and late August of YR-01, I drove back and forth between Bald Mountain, Alabama, and Madison, Wisconsin, three or four times in order to move my belongings to Madison. I traveled to Bald Mountain, Alabama, from December 21, YR-01 to January 3, YR-00, in order to celebrate the holidays with my siblings who still live in Bald Mountain and engage counsel for the purpose of bringing this lawsuit. I traveled to Bald Mountain from June 6 though June 12, YR-00, during which time I visited friends and family and attended my niece's baptism. On each occasion I stayed at the home of my brother, Joseph Petrillo.

Interrogatory No. 8: For any and all driver's licenses that you have held, identify the state and date of issue.

Answer: I obtained an Alabama driver's license in June of YR-8. I surrendered that license in October of YR-01, when I obtained a Wisconsin driver's license.

Interrogatory No. 9: For any and all motor vehicles that you possess, identify where you purchased the vehicle, the state(s) of registration and the date on which the vehicle was first registered in that state(s).

Answer: I have a YR-6 Honda Civic, which I purchased in Birmingham, Alabama, in August of YR-06 and registered at that time in Alabama. In October YR-01, I registered the vehicle in Wisconsin.

Interrogatory No. 10: In what state, if any, have you paid state or local taxes for the years YR-25 through the present?

Answer: I paid income taxes in Alabama for the years YR-06 through YR-01. I moved to Wisconsin in the middle of YR-01, but had Alabama income for the first half of that year. I paid a portion of property taxes on property owned jointly with my siblings in Alabama for the year s YR-02 and YR-01. I have not had income since moving to Wisconsin, and have not therefore yet paid any income taxes or other taxes in Wisconsin.

Interrogatory No. 11: Do you have any specific occupational plans after completion of your studies at the University of Wisconsin?

Answer: I have no definite plans. I intend to seek a position as a librarian.

Interrogatory No. 12: Do you have any specific occupational commitments or job offers in Wisconsin for after completion of your studies at the University of Wisconsin?

Answer: No.

Interrogatory No. 13: Have you ever been employed in Wisconsin?

Answer: No.

Interrogatory No. 14: Identify all immediate family members and their place of residence.

Answer: My sister Mary Petrillo resides in Madison, Wisconsin. My brother Joseph Petrillo and his wife, my sister-in-law Jennifer Petrillo, reside in Bald Mountain, Alabama. My sister Rachel Petrillo resides in Bald Mountain, Alabama.

Interrogatory No. 15: Other than facts set forth in the Complaint or elsewhere in these interrogatory answers, identify all facts upon which you rely to claim a change of domicile from Alabama to Wisconsin.

Answer: I reside in Madison, Wisconsin, where I have leased an apartment. Other than a trust fund established by my parents prior to their deaths, I am the sole source of my own support. I have no plans to move back to Alabama. Upon completion of my post-graduate studies, I intend to seek employment as a librarian in Wisconsin or elsewhere.

Dated: February 21, YR-00

Armand DuPriest
_____

Armand DuPriest
Wilson & DuPriest
900 Maple Lane
Bald Mountain, Alabama 36918
Attorney for the plaintiff,
Ernestine Petrillo

VERIFICATION

I, Ernestine Petrillo, the undersigned, declare and state:

I am the plaintiff in this action.

I have read the foregoing Plaintiff's Answer to Defendants' Interrogatories. Based on my personal knowledge, the answers stated therein are true and correct.

I declare under penalty of perjury under the laws of the United States that the foregoing is true and correct.

Executed on February 19, YR-00, in Madison, Wisconsin.

Ernestine Petrillo
_____
Ernestine Petrillo

PROOF OF SERVICE

I certify that on this 21st day of February, YR-00, I served the foregoing Plaintiff's Answers to Defendants' Interrogatories upon the defendants by causing a copy thereof to be delivered by hand to counsel for the defendants, Emily Rumsdale, Esquire, Miller, Eldridge & Pasternak, 13304 Bald Mountain Parkway, Bald Mountain, Alabama 36918.

Armand DuPriest
_____
Armand DuPriest

Wilson & DuPriest
900 Maple Lane
Bald Mountain, Alabama 36918
Telephone: (934) 444-2541

Attorney for the Plaintiff
Ernestine Petrillo

IN THE UNITED STATES DISTRICT COURT
FOR THE WESTERN DISTRICT OF ALABAMA

ERNESTINE PETRILLO

 PLAINTIFF

VS.

LINWOOD ROOKS, ET AL.

 DEFENDANTS

```
┌─────────────────────────────────┐
│  UNITED STATES DISTRICT COURT   │
│            FILED                │
│      April 2, YR-00             │
│  WESTERN DISTRICT OF ALABAMA    │
└─────────────────────────────────┘
```

CIVIL ACTION NO. 00-85FD

DEPOSITION OF HARRIETT YUN

TAKEN BY PLAINTIFF AT 900 MAPLE LANE, BALD MOUNTAIN, ALABAMA,
COMMENCING AT 10:00 A.M., MARCH 30, YR-00, BEFORE LEONARD AHERN,
OFFICIAL COURT REPORTER

APPEARANCES:

 FOR PLAINTIFF:

  WILSON & DUPRIEST

   BY: ARMAND DUPRIEST, ESQ.

  900 MAPLE LANE
  BALD MOUNTAIN, ALABAMA 36918
  TELEPHONE (934) 333-2541

 FOR DEFENDANTS HARRIETT YUN AND BALD MOUNTAIN COMMUNITY CHURCH:

  MILLER, ELDRIDGE & PASTERNAK

   BY: EMILY RUMSDALE, ESQ.

  13304 BALD MOUNTAIN PARKWAY
  BALD MOUNTAIN, ALABAMA 36918
  TELEPHONE (934) 485-9000

[Document page 1]

1   BALD MOUNTAIN, ALABAMA, MARCH 30, YR-00

2   HARRIETT YUN

3   HAVING BEEN DULY SWORN, TESTIFIED AS FOLLOWS:

4   EXAMINATION

5   BY MR. DUPRIEST:

6   MY NAME IS ARMAND DUPRIEST. I REPRESENT ERNESTINE PETRILLO IN

7 CIVIL ACTION NO. 00-85 IN THE UNITED STATES DISTRICT COURT FOR THE

8 WESTERN DISTRICT OF ALABAMA. THIS MORNING I SHALL BE TAKING THE

9 DEPOSITION OF HARRIETT YUN, ONE OF THE DEFENDANTS IN THAT ACTION.

10 MAY THE RECORD REFLECT THAT MS. YUN IS PRESENT WITH HER ATTORNEY,

11 MS. EMILY RUMSDALE, AND WE ARE JOINED BY THE COURT REPORTER, MR.

12 AHERN.

13   Q   GOOD MORNING, MS. YUN.   FOR THE RECORD WOULD YOU PLEASE STATE

14 YOUR FULL NAME AND PLEASE SPELL YOUR NAME?

15   A   HARRIET YUN, H-A-R-R-I-E-T-T Y-U-N.

16   Q   THAT'S REVEREND YUN, CORRECT?

17   A   MOST FOLKS CALL ME PASTOR YUN, BUT REVEREND YUN IS

18 ACCEPTABLE.

19   Q   PASTOR YUN, YOU HAVE BEEN NAMED AS ONE OF THE DEFENDANTS IN

20 THIS ACTION, IS THAT CORRECT?

21   A   YES.

22   Q   AND YOU ARE ACCOMPANIED TODAY BY YOUR ATTORNEY, MS. RUMSDALE?

23   A   THAT'S CORRECT.

24   Q   PASTOR YUN, HAVE YOU HAD YOUR DEPOSITION TAKEN BEFORE?

25   A   MAYBE TWO OR THREE TIMES IN CONNECTION WITH FAMILY DISPUTES

26 INVOLVING MEMBERS OF MY CONGREGATION.

27   Q   YOU UNDERSTAND THAT THE PURPOSE OF THIS DEPOSITION IS TO

1 DISCOVER YOUR TESTIMONY FOR USE IN THE CASE OF ERNESTINE PETRILLO

2 VERSUS LINWOOD ROOKS, BALD MOUNTAIN COMMUNITY CHURCH, AND YOURSELF,

3 HARRIETT YUN?

4   A   YES.

5   Q   AND YOU ARE HERE TODAY BECAUSE OF AN ORDER OF THE UNITED

6 STATES DISTRICT COURT THAT YOUR DEPOSITION BE TAKEN IN THAT ACTION

7 TODAY?

8   A   YES, THAT'S MY UNDERSTANDING. MS. RUMSDALE TOLD ME THAT I

9 SHOULD BE HERE THIS MORNING TO GIVE A DEPOSITION.

10   Q   AND YOU UNDERSTAND TODAY THAT YOU ARE UNDER OATH TO TELL THE

11 TRUTH AND THAT IF YOU DO NOT TELL THE TRUTH YOU MAY BE LIABLE TO

12 PROSECUTION FOR THE OFFENSE OF PERJURY, DO YOU UNDERSTAND THAT?

13   A   YES, I DO.

14   Q   AND YOU HAVE TAKEN AN OATH TO TELL THE TRUTH AND IT IS YOUR

15 OBLIGATION TO TELL THE TRUTH AND NOTHING BUT THE TRUTH, DO YOU

16 UNDERSTAND THAT?

17   A   OF COURSE.

18   Q   DO YOU HAVE ANY MENTAL RESERVATIONS ABOUT YOUR OATH TO TELL

19 THE TRUTH, THE WHOLE TRUTH, AND NOTHING BUT THE TRUTH?

20   A   NOT AT ALL.

21   Q   IN YOUR TESTIMONY TODAY I WILL BE ASKING YOU SOME QUESTIONS

22 AND MS. RUMSDALE MAY BE ASKING YOU SOME QUESTIONS, AND IF AT ANY

23 POINT YOU DO NOT UNDERSTAND A QUESTION, PLEASE LET US KNOW THAT YOU

24 DON'T UNDERSTAND THE QUESTION AND WE WILL TRY TO CLARIFY IT FOR YOU.

25 WILL YOU DO THAT?

26   A   CERTAINLY.

27   Q   AND IF AT ANY POINT ONE OF THE LAWYERS OBJECTS TO A QUESTION,

[Document page 3]

1   PLEASE JUST HOLD YOUR ANSWER UNTIL THE OBJECTION HAS BEEN FULLY

2   STATED AND THE LAWYERS CAN DISCUSS WHETHER YOU WILL BE ALLOWED TO

3   ANSWER THE QUESTION. WILL YOU DO THAT?

4   A   YES.

5   Q   FOR THE RECORD, HOW IS YOUR HEALTH?

6   A   MY HEALTH IS EXCELLENT, THANK YOU.

7   Q   YOU ARE FEELING OK, NOT COMING DOWN WITH ANYTHING?

8   A   I'M FEELING VERY WELL, THANK YOU.

9   Q   THE NEXT QUESTION IS STRICTLY ROUTINE. NO OFFENSE INTENDED.

10   AND THAT IS ARE YOU UNDER THE INFLUENCE OF ALCOHOL OR ANY NARCOTICS

11   OR STIMULANTS OR ANY OTHER DRUG OR SUBSTANCE WHATSOEVER?

12   A   NO OFFENSE TAKEN. NO, I DO NOT USE ALCOHOL OR DRUGS OTHER

13   THAN PRESCRIPTION MEDICATIONS.

14   Q   WHAT PRESCRIPTION MEDICATIONS DO YOU TAKE?

15   A   I TAKE MEDICINE TO HELP BRING DOWN MY CHOLESTEROL AND

16   SOMETIMES I TAKE A PILL TO HELP ME SLEEP.

17   Q   DO THOSE MEDICATIONS AFFECT YOUR ALERTNESS OR MENTAL

18   FUNCTIONING?

19   A   WELL, THE SLEEPING PILL MAKES ME SLEEPY, BUT NOT THE

20   CHOLESTEROL MEDICINE.

21   Q   WHEN IS THE LAST TIME YOU TOOK A SLEEPING PILL?

22   A   OH, IT MUST HAVE BEEN TWO OR THREE WEEKS AGO. DO YOU NEED TO

23   KNOW EXACTLY?

24   Q   I DON'T THINK SO. YOU'RE FEELING ALERT THIS MORNING?

25   A   BRIGHT EYED AND BUSHY TAILED. THAT'S ME.

26   Q   CAN YOU THINK OF ANY REASON WHY YOU SHOULD NOT HAVE YOUR

27   TESTIMONY TAKEN THIS MORNING?

[Document page 4]

1   A   NO.

2   Q   ARE YOU AWARE OF ANY REASON WHY YOU WILL NOT BE ABLE TO FULLY

3   AND TRUTHFULLY ANSWER ALL MY QUESTIONS THIS MORNING?

4   A   NO.

5   Q   PASTOR YUN, COULD YOU TELL US HOW YOU CAME TO BE ASSOCIATED

6   WITH BALD MOUNTAIN COMMUNITY CHURCH?

7   A   ACTUALLY, I FOUNDED THE CHURCH ALONG WITH A HANDFUL OF THE

8   FAITHFUL WHO WERE DRAWN TO MY MINISTRY. I GREW UP IN BALD MOUNTAIN

9   AND HAVE LIVED HERE ALL MY LIFE EXCEPT WHEN I WAS IN COLLEGE AND

10   SEMINARY AND FOR A COUPLE OF YEARS AFTER SEMINARY. WHEN I RETURNED

11   TO BALD MOUNTAIN IT WAS WITH AN ACUTE AWARENESS OF THE LIMITED

12   CHOICES FOR CHRISTIAN WORSHIP AND FELLOWSHIP IN THIS COMMUNITY. AT

13   THAT TIME, THE ONLY CHURCHES IN BALD MOUNTAIN WERE OF THE

14   HIERARCHICAL DENOMINATIONS LIKE ROMAN CATHOLIC, EPISCOPAL,

15   METHODIST, AND LUTHERAN. WHY, THERE WASN'T EVEN A BAPTIST OR A

16   CONGREGATIONAL CHURCH HERE. YET THERE WERE MANY FAMILIES IN THIS

17   COMMUNITY THAT WANTED TO BE PART OF AN INDEPENDENT CHURCH, ONE THAT

18   WAS NOT ANSWERABLE TO ANYONE EXCEPT THE ALMIGHTY ACTING THROUGH THE

19   CONGREGATION. ONE THING LED TO ANOTHER. I STARTED CONDUCTING

20   WORSHIP SERVICES IN PRIVATE HOMES IN YR-24. IN YR-20 OUR

21   CONGREGATION SCRAPED TOGETHER SUFFICIENT FUNDS TO PURCHASE A SMALL

22   EXISTING CHURCH BUILDING THAT HAD BEEN ABANDONED BY A LUTHERAN

23   CONGREGATION. AT THAT POINT, WE ORGANIZED THE CHURCH FORMALLY, WITH

24   AN ELECTED CHURCH COUNCIL, OFFICERS, AND THE LIKE. THE CONGREGATION

25   CALLED ME TO ASSUME THE TITLE OF SENIOR PASTOR, AND I HAVE CONTINUED

26   WITH GOD'S HELP TO LEAD THE CHURCH EVER SINCE. THE CHURCH HAS GROWN

27   TREMENDOUSLY. WE BUILT A MAGNIFICENT NEW WORSHIP AND EDUCATIONAL

[Document page 5]

1   COMPLEX ALONG WITH FIRST CLASS RECREATIONAL FACILITIES FOR THE YOUNG

2   PEOPLE.   THAT WAS IN YR-13 AND YR-12. AND THEN -- OH DEAR, I'M

3   AFRAID I'M RAMBLING ON.   DID I ANSWER YOUR QUESTION?

4   Q   YES, INDEED. COULD YOU DESCRIBE THE CHURCH AS IT IS TODAY?

5   HOW LARGE IS THE CONGREGATION? THE MINISTERIAL STAFF?

6   A   THE LAST TIME I LOOKED, THE MEMBERSHIP WAS APPROACHING 3,000.

7   IN ADDITION TO MYSELF AS SENIOR PASTOR, WE HAVE FIVE ASSOCIATE AND

8   ASSISTANT PASTORS, A DIRECTOR OF EDUCATION, A DIRECTOR OF MUSIC, AN

9   ORGANIST AND A CHOIR DIRECTOR, AND WE ALSO HAVE AN OFFICE STAFF AND

10 A HALF DOZEN CUSTODIANS AND GROUNDSKEEPERS.

11   Q   IS THE GOVERNANCE OF THE CHURCH STILL THE SAME AS YOU

12 DESCRIBED IT IN YR-20?

13   A   BASICALLY. STILL AN ELECTED CHURCH COUNCIL, ALTHOUGH MAJOR

14 DECISIONS ARE MADE DIRECTLY BY THE CONGREGATION IN QUARTERLY

15 BUSINESS MEETINGS. AND AS THE CHURCH HAS GROWN, MORE AND MORE

16 COMMITTEES AND SPECIAL GROUPS HAVE EMERGED.   BUT THE BASIC

17 GOVERNANCE IS THAT THE CONGREGATION ELECTS THE COUNCIL AND THE

18 COUNCIL RUNS THE PLACE AS BEST IT CAN WITHOUT GETTING IN GOD'S WAY.

19   Q   IS YOUR CHURCH AFFILIATED WITH ANY OTHER CHURCHES?

20   A   WE ARE A MEMBER OF A NATIONAL ORGANIZATION OF COMMUNITY

21 CHURCHES AND OF SEVERAL SOCIAL SERVICE ORGANIZATIONS. NONE OF THOSE

22 ORGANIZATIONS HAS ANY AUTHORITY TO GOVERN BALD MOUNTAIN COMMUNITY

23 CHURCH, TO REVIEW DECISIONS OF OUR CHURCH, TO DISCIPLINE THE CLERGY,

24 OR TO PRESCRIBE DOCTRINE.

25   Q   WHAT IS THE PROCESS FOR HIRING MEMBERS OF THE MINISTERIAL

26 STAFF?

27   A   ON RECOMMENDATION OF THE SENIOR PASTOR AND THE CHURCH

[Document page 6]

1 COUNCIL, THE CONGREGATION DECIDES THAT IT WANTS TO REPLACE AN

2 ASSOCIATE OR ASSISTANT PASTOR WHO HAS MOVED ON OR TO CREATE A NEW

3 PASTORAL POSITION. WHEN THAT IS DECIDED, THE CONGREGATION APPOINTS A

4 CALL COMMITTEE. IN RECENT YEARS THE CONGREGATION HAS SIMPLY

5 DESIGNATED THE CHURCH COUNCIL TO SERVE AS A CALL COMMITTEE. THE

6 CALL COMMITTEE GOES THROUGH A PROCESS OF SEARCHING FOR QUALIFIED

7 INDIVIDUALS, INVITES APPLICATIONS, SCREENS THOSE APPLICATIONS,

8 CHECKS REFERENCES, AND GRADUALLY IDENTIFIES A SMALL GROUP OF

9 POSSIBILITIES WHO ARE INVITED TO VISIT AND WORSHIP WITH US SO WE CAN

10 GET TO KNOW THEM AND THEY CAN PRAYERFULLY LISTEN TO GOD'S VOICE AND

11 HEAR A CALLING. IN THE USUAL CASE THE CALL COMMITTEE WILL RECOMMEND

12 ONE INDIVIDUAL TO THE CONGREGATION, AND THE CONGREGATION WILL HOLD A

13 SPECIAL MEETING, REVIEW ALL OF THE INFORMATION AND IMPRESSIONS FROM

14 THE CANDIDATE'S VISIT, AND DECIDE WHETHER TO ISSUE A CALL.

15   Q   DO MEMBERS OF THE MINISTERIAL STAFF HAVE SPECIAL ASSIGNMENTS

16 OR INDIVIDUALIZED RESPONSIBILITIES?

17   A   MOST DO.   PARTICULAR ASSOCIATE AND ASSISTANT PASTORS MAY BE

18 RESPONSIBLE FOR VISITATION, EDUCATION, YOUTH PROGRAMS, COUNSELING

19 AND THE LIKE.   ALL OF OUR PASTORS REGULARLY PARTICIPATE IN WORSHIP

20 SERVICES. WE HAVE NINE OR TEN WORSHIP SERVICES EVERY WEEK.

21   Q   HAS THE CHURCH ALWAYS HAD A FACILITY FOR PASTORAL COUNSELING?

22   A   COUNSELING HAS BEEN ONE OF MY PRIMARY INTERESTS SINCE THE

23 BEGINNING OF MY MINISTRY. IT WAS ONE OF MY MAIN ACTIVITIES DURING

24 THE EARLY DAYS OF OUR CHURCH HERE IN BALD MOUNTAIN. FROM TIME TO

25 TIME, ONE OR ANOTHER OF THE ASSOCIATE PASTORS DOES COUNSELING. IT

26 IS FUNDAMENTAL TO OUR CONCEPT OF THE PASTORAL ROLE. IN YR-11 WE

27 DECIDED THAT WE NEEDED TO ADD AN ASSOCIATE PASTOR WHO WAS

[Document page 7]

1 SPECIFICALLY TRAINED IN COUNSELING AND WHOSE FULL TIME WOULD BE

2 DEVOTED TO THAT FUNCTION. AND THAT IS WHAT WE DID. SINCE THEN THE

3 CHURCH HAS MAINTAINED A PASTORAL COUNSELING CENTER THAT IS OPEN NOT

4 ONLY TO OUR CONGREGATION BUT TO ANYONE IN THE COMMUNITY WHO IS

5 SEEKING A RELIGIOUSLY ORIENTED COUNSELING EXPERIENCE. WE HAVE HAD

6 THREE DIFFERENT ASSOCIATE PASTORS FOR COUNSELING. THE FIRST WAS

7 CALLED IN YR-11 AND LEFT IN YR-05 TO TAKE A POSITION WITH A

8 NATIONALLY RANKED PASTORAL COUNSELING CENTER IN CHICAGO. THE NEXT

9 ASSOCIATE PASTOR FOR COUNSELING WAS NOT WITH US VERY LONG. HE WAS

10 RELIEVED OF HIS DUTIES IN JANUARY YR-03. AFTER THAT IS WHEN REV.

11 ROOKS JOINED US.

12   Q   I TAKE IT YOU ARE REFERRING TO LINWOOD ROOKS, ONE OF THE

13 DEFENDANTS IN THIS ACTION?

14   A   THAT'S RIGHT.

15   Q   WHAT WAS THE PROCESS BY WHICH REV. ROOKS WAS HIRED? HOW DID

16 YOU FIND HIM, OR DID HE COME TO YOU LOOKING FOR A JOB?

17   A   THE GENERAL PROCESS WAS THE PROCESS I DESCRIBED A FEW MOMENTS

18 AGO. THE CONGREGATION AUTHORIZED A SEARCH IN FEBRUARY YR-03 AND

19 APPOINTED THE CHURCH COUNCIL TO SERVE AS THE CALL COMMITTEE. MS.

20 EPPERSON, WHO WAS CHAIR OF THE CHURCH COUNCIL, ASKED ME TO HELP

21 IDENTIFY QUALIFIED CANDIDATES. I PHONED MY OLD FRIEND AND

22 COLLEAGUE, LELAND LAMPREY NORTH, TO SEE IF HE KNEW SOMEONE WHO MIGHT

23 FIT OUR NEEDS. DR. NORTH IS THE DIRECTOR OF A COUNSELING CENTER AND

24 TEACHING FACILITY IN NASHVILLE. WHEN I TOLD HIM ABOUT OUR SEARCH, HE

25 IMMEDIATELY MENTIONED LINWOOD ROOKS. ROOKS WAS APPROACHING THE END

26 OF A THREE YEAR INTERNSHIP WITH DR. NORTH'S PROGRAM AND NORTH WAS

27 VERY HIGH ON HIM. ON THE BASIS OF DR. NORTH'S RECOMMENDATION, I

[Document page 8]

1 SUGGESTED TO MS. EPPERSON THAT THE CALL COMMITTEE MIGHT WANT TO

2 CONSIDER REV. ROOKS. HE VISITED AND INTERVIEWED WITH US IN MARCH OF

3 THAT YEAR, AND IN MAY THE CONGREGATION VOTED TO CALL REV. ROOKS TO

4 BE OUR ASSOCIATE PASTOR FOR COUNSELING. HE JOINED US ON JULY 1, YR-

5 03.

6   Q   WHAT INVESTIGATION DID YOU OR ANYONE ELSE MAKE OF REV. ROOKS'

7 BACKGROUND AND EXPERIENCE?

8   A   I RELIED ENTIRELY ON THE RECOMMENDATION OF LELAND LAMPREY

9 NORTH. HE IS A WISE AND KNOWLEDGEABLE PERSON WHOSE JUDGMENT I TRUST

10 IMPLICITLY. HE SAID ROOKS HAD PERFORMED EXTREMELY WELL IN HIS

11 INTERNSHIP AND WAS NOW READY TO TAKE ON AN INDEPENDENT ROLE AS A

12 PASTORAL COUNSELOR.

13   Q   DID YOU ASK DR. NORTH WHETHER HE HAD HEARD ANY COMPLAINTS

14 ABOUT REV. ROOKS?

15   A   NOT SPECIFICALLY. I AM SURE IT WOULD HAVE COME OUT IF THERE

16 HAD BEEN.

17   Q   DID YOU ASK ABOUT HIS PROFESSIONAL ETHICS AS A COUNSELOR?

18   A   AGAIN, IT WOULD HAVE COME OUT IF THERE WAS A PROBLEM. I DID

19 NOT SPECIFICALLY ASK.

20   Q   DID DR. NORTH TELL YOU THAT ON MORE THAN ONE OCCASION HE HAD

21 LEARNED THAT REV. ROOKS WAS ATTEMPTING TO PROMOTE BUSINESS VENTURES

22 WITH CLIENTS AND WAS TRYING TO GET CLIENTS TO INVEST IN BUSINESS

23 SCHEMES THAT ROOKS HAD COME UP WITH?

24   A   NO. NOTHING LIKE THAT.

25   Q   WHAT DID YOU SAY IS THE NAME OF THE PERSON WHO CHAIRS THE

26 CHURCH COUNCIL?

27   A   LAURA BELLE EPPERSON.

[Document page 9]

1   Q   DID LAURA BELLE EPPERSON DO ANY BACKGROUND CHECK OR OTHER

2 INQUIRY ABOUT REV. ROOKS?

3   A   NOT THAT I AM AWARE OF. I THINK SHE AND THE REST OF THE

4 COUNCIL WERE SATISFIED WITH THE STRONG RECOMMENDATION THAT I PASSED

5 ALONG TO THEM FROM DR. NORTH. I DON'T KNOW EVERYTHING THEY DID, BUT

6 SHE NEVER SAID ANYTHING TO ME ABOUT THEIR CHECKING REV. ROOKS'

7 REFERENCES.

8   Q   WHAT QUALIFICATIONS DID MR. ROOKS HAVE OTHER THAN DR. NORTH'S

9 RECOMMENDATION?

10   A   AS I RECALL, HE HAD GRADUATED FROM SEMINARY AND EARNED A

11 MASTERS OF DIVINITY DEGREE. AFTER BEING ORDAINED, HE ENTERED A

12 GRADUATE PROGRAM IN PASTORAL COUNSELING, WHERE HE EARNED A DOCTORAL

13 DEGREE. AND THEN HE HAD NEARLY COMPLETED A DEMANDING INTERNSHIP

14 UNDER ONE OF THIS COUNTRY'S LEADING EXPERTS. IN ADDITION TO ALL

15 THAT, ALL OF US WHO WERE INVOLVED IN THE DECISION TO CALL HIM

16 EXPERIENCED HIM AS A WARM, CARING, AND EMPATHETIC SOUL. WE FOUND HIM

17 TO BE EXTREMELY WELL TRAINED AND EMINENTLY QUALIFIED.

18   Q   DID YOU OR ANY MEMBER OF THE CHURCH CHECK ANY REFERENCES FOR

19 MR. ROOKS OTHER THAN YOUR CONVERSATION WITH DR. NORTH?

20   A   NOT TO MY KNOWLEDGE. I DIDN'T.

21   Q   DID YOU RUN A CRIMINAL RECORDS CHECK OR ATTEMPT TO DETERMINE

22 WHETHER HE HAD BEEN INVOLVED IN LITIGATION OR IN ANY DISCIPLINARY

23 MATTERS WHILE IN COLLEGE AND GRADUATE SCHOOLS?

24   A   I DON'T THINK SO.

25   Q   SINCE HE BEGAN AS ASSOCIATE PASTOR FOR COUNSELING AT BALD

26 MOUNTAIN COMMUNITY CHURCH, WHO HAS BEEN LINWOOD ROOKS' SUPERVISOR?

27   A   AS THE SENIOR PASTOR, I HAVE ULTIMATE SUPERVISORY AUTHORITY

1 AND RESPONSIBILITY FOR THE ASSOCIATE AND ASSISTANT PASTORS. HOWEVER,

2 I SHOULD POINT OUT THAT WE ARE A PRETTY AUTONOMOUS BUNCH.   EACH OF

3 US HAS HIS OR HER UNIQUE CALLING, AND IT IS NOT FOR ME OR ANYONE

4 ELSE TO SAY HOW A FELLOW SERVANT OF GOD SHOULD PURSUE THAT CALLING.

5   Q   DURING MR. ROOKS' TENURE AS ASSOCIATE PASTOR FOR COUNSELING,

6 WHO SET OFFICE HOURS, INTAKE POLICIES, AND BILLING POLICIES OF THE

7 PASTORAL COUNSELING CENTER?

8   A   REV. ROOKS DID. THAT WAS HIS JOB.

9   Q   DID HE EVER DISCUSS ANY OF THOSE MATTERS WITH YOU?

10   A   WELL, THE CHURCH BUDGET HAS LINE ITEMS FOR VARIOUS INCOME AND

11 EXPENSE ITEMS ATTRIBUTABLE TO THE PASTORAL COUNSELING CENTER, AND I

12 MADE SURE THAT REV. ROOKS WAS FAMILIAR WITH THOSE AND COULD LIVE

13 WITH THEM.   OTHERWISE, THE ANSWER IS NO.

14   Q   DID YOU OR ANYONE ELSE CONDUCT PERIODIC REVIEWS OF HIS WORK?

15   A   NO, THAT WOULD HAVE BEEN INAPPROPRIATE.

16   Q   HOW SO?

17   A   REV. ROOKS WAS NOT A GROUNDSKEEPER OR A CLERICAL STAFF.   HE

18 WAS A PROFESSIONAL PERSON AND INDIVIDUALLY ORDAINED IN HIS OWN RIGHT

19 AS A MINISTER OF THE GOSPEL. I WOULD NOT PRESUME TO GO AROUND ASKING

20 HIM TO FILL OUT FORMS AND GIVE ME REPORTS ABOUT HIS MINISTRY.

21   Q   DID YOU EVER HEAR ANYTHING ADVERSE ABOUT HIS WORK AS

22 ASSOCIATE PASTOR FOR COUNSELING AT BALD MOUNTAIN COMMUNITY CHURCH?

23   A   NOT UNTIL MS. PETRILLO COMPLAINED TO ME.

24   Q   WHEN WAS THAT?

25   A   SOMETIME IN MAY OF LAST YEAR.

26   Q   WHAT WAS HER COMPLAINT?

27   A   BASICALLY THAT HE HAD DUPED HER INTO SOME FOOLISH INVESTMENTS

[Document page 11]

1   INVOLVING A COMPANY IN WHICH REV. ROOKS WAS FINANCIALLY INTERESTED.

2   Q   WHAT WAS YOUR REACTION TO THAT COMPLAINT?

3   A   I WAS EXTREMELY CONCERNED AND DISAPPOINTED. I CONFRONTED

4   LINWOOD AND HE DECIDED ALMOST IMMEDIATELY TO TAKE A LEAVE OF

5   ABSENCE. A COUPLE OF MONTHS LATER HE RESIGNED AS ASSOCIATE PASTOR.

6   THAT WAS ONLY A FEW WEEKS BEFORE THE CRIMINAL CHARGES WERE FILED

7   AGAINST HIM.

8   Q   HAD YOU EVER HEARD ANYTHING LIKE THIS AT ANY TIME PRIOR TO

9   MAY OF LAST YEAR?

10   A   NOT EXACTLY.

11   Q   WHAT DOES THAT MEAN?

12   A   I AM NOT AT LIBERTY TO DISCLOSE SOME INFORMATION TO WHICH I

13 AM PRIVY.

14   Q   WHY IS THAT?

15   A   AS A PASTOR, I AM THE REPOSITORY OF MANY FOLKS' CONFIDENCES,

16 WHICH I CANNOT DISCLOSE.

17   Q   DOES THAT INCLUDE INFORMATION PROVIDED TO YOU BY ESTHER

18 BORZOI?

19   A   I AM NOT AT LIBERTY TO SAY.

20   Q   DO YOU KNOW ESTHER BORZOI?

21   A   YES.

22   Q   HOW DO YOU KNOW HER?

23   A   SHE HAS BEEN A MEMBER OF OUR CONGREGATION FOR THREE OR FOUR

24 YEARS AND FROM TIME TO TIME SHE HAS DONE PART-TIME WORK IN THE

25 CHURCH OFFICE.

26   Q   WHAT KIND OF WORK?

27   A   ANSWERING THE PHONES, FILING, GENERAL CLERICAL WORK.

[Document page 12]

1   Q   HAVE YOU HAD CONVERSATIONS WITH ESTHER BORZOI?

2   A   YES.

3   Q   DID YOU HAVE A CONVERSATION WITH HER IN DECEMBER YR-03,

4   APPROXIMATELY IN THE SECOND WEEK OF DECEMBER?

5   A   YES.

6   Q   WHAT DID YOU DISCUSS?

7   A   I AM NOT AT LIBERTY TO SAY.

8   Q   UNDER WHAT CIRCUMSTANCES DID THIS CONVERSATION OCCUR?

9   A   ESTHER CAME TO ME IN MY STUDY AT THE CHURCH AND SAID SHE

10   NEEDED TO TALK WITH ME. I INVITED HER TO SIT DOWN AND WE CONVERSED.

11   Q   DID ESTHER SAY ANYTHING TO INDICATE THAT SHE INTENDED THIS

12   CONVERSATION TO BE CONFIDENTIAL?

13   A   OH, YES. SHE SPECIFICALLY TOLD ME THAT SHE WANTED OUR

14   CONVERSATION TO BE CONFIDENTIAL.

15   Q   DID SHE MAKE A CONFESSION TO YOU? WAS SHE SEEKING

16   ABSOLUTION?

17   A   THOSE ARE CONCEPTS THAT ARE ALIEN TO MY BELIEF SYSTEM, AND I

18   DON'T THINK THAT WOULD BE A FAIR DESCRIPTION OF OUR CONVERSATION.

19   Q   DID SHE SEEK SPIRITUAL ADVICE AND COMFORT?

20   A   I WOULD SAY YES.

21   Q   ISN'T IT TRUE THAT WHAT SHE TOLD YOU SHE HAD LEARNED IN HER

22   CAPACITY AS AN EMPLOYEE AND SHE WAS AFRAID OF GETTING IN TROUBLE IN

23   CONNECTION WITH HER WORK?

24   A   I AM NOT AT LIBERTY TO SAY.

25   Q   ISN'T IT TRUE THAT ESTHER BORZOI TOLD YOU THAT SHE HAD HEARD

26   FROM AT LEAST TWO PEOPLE WHO WERE CLIENTS IN PASTORAL COUNSELING OF

27   REV. ROOKS THAT MR. ROOKS WAS URGING THEM TO INVEST IN A BED AND

1   BREAKFAST BUSINESS THAT HE WAS STARTING UP?

2   A   MR. DUPRIEST, THAT'S STRIKING RIGHT AT THE HEART OF MY

3   OBLIGATION TO KEEP THE SECRETS AND CONFIDENCES THAT MEMBERS OF MY

4   CHURCH ENTRUST TO ME. I REFUSE TO ANSWER THAT QUESTION.

5   MS. RUMSDALE: LET ME SAY FOR THE RECORD THAT PASTOR YUN BASES

6   HER REFUSAL TO ANSWER QUESTIONS ABOUT CONFIDENCES ENTRUSTED TO HER

7   ON THE MINISTERIAL PRIVILEGE SET FORTH IN RULE 505 OF THE ALABAMA

8   RULES OF EVIDENCE.

9   BY MR. DUPRIEST:

10   Q   IS THAT CORRECT, REV. YUN?

11   A   YES.

12   Q   I ALSO INTENDED TO ASK YOU WHETHER MS. BORZOI HAD MENTIONED

13 TO YOU A CONVERSATION THAT SHE HAD WITH REV. ROOKS ON THE SUBJECT OF

14 HIS BED AND BREAKFAST BUSINESS AND ANOTHER CONVERSATION THAT SHE HAD

15 WITH AN ASSISTANT PASTOR, WHO TOLD MS. BORZOI THAT HE HAD HEARD

16 COMPLAINTS ABOUT MR. ROOKS' MIXING PERSONAL BUSINESS WITH

17 COUNSELING. WOULD I BE CORRECT IN ASSUMING THAT YOU WOULD REFUSE TO

18 ANSWER THOSE QUESTIONS FOR THE SAME REASONS?

19   A   YES.

20   Q   PASTOR YUN, DID YOU HAVE A CONVERSATION WITH MS. BORZOI ON

21 AUGUST 26 OF LAST YEAR, YR-01?

22   A   YES.

23   Q   DID SHE TELL YOU IN THAT CONVERSATION THAT SHE NO LONGER

24 REGARDS HER CONVERSATION WITH YOU IN THE SECOND WEEK OF DECEMBER,

25 YR-03, TO BE CONFIDENTIAL?

26   A   SHE DID SAY THAT.

27   Q   AND THAT SHE DOES NOT OBJECT TO YOUR REVEALING WHAT SHE SAID

1   TO YOU?

2   A   THAT IS WHAT SHE SAID.

3   Q   KNOWING THAT MS. BORZOI NO LONGER WISHES THAT CONVERSATION TO

4   BE KEPT SECRET, WOULD YOU NOW BE WILLING TO ANSWER MY PREVIOUS

5   QUESTIONS ABOUT YOUR CONVERSATION WITH HER IN DECEMBER YR-03?

6   A   NO. I CANNOT REVEAL SECRETS THAT WERE ORIGINALLY ENTRUSTED

7   TO ME IN CONFIDENCE IN MY ROLE AS A MINISTER OF THE GOSPEL SIMPLY

8   BECAUSE THE OTHER PERSON CHANGES HER MIND.

9   Q   FOLLOWING YOUR CONVERSATION WITH MS. BORZOI IN DECEMBER YR-

10 03, DID IT OCCUR TO YOU THAT THERE WAS SOME HANKY-PANKY GOING ON AND

11 THAT YOU HAD A RESPONSIBILITY TO STEP UP TO PREVENT INNOCENT AND

12 VULNERABLE PEOPLE FROM BEING EXPLOITED?

13   MS. RUMSDALE: I MUST OBJECT TO THAT QUESTION AS ARGUMENTATIVE.

14 ALSO, IT IS ATTEMPTING TO SECURE BY INDIRECTION WHAT YOU CANNOT GET

15 DIRECTLY, NAMELY TO REVEAL WHAT MS. BORZOI MAY HAVE TOLD HER IN

16 CONFIDENCE. I WILL DIRECT THE WITNESS NOT TO ANSWER THAT QUESTION.

17   MR. DUPRIEST: COUNSEL, I TOTALLY DISAGREE WITH YOUR POSITION AND

18 I SEE NO BASIS FOR INVOKING THE RULE 505 PRIVILEGE TO CONCEAL THE

19 FACT THAT YOUR CLIENT WAS ON NOTICE OF MR. ROOKS' SHENANIGANS WHEN

20 IT WOULD HAVE STILL BEEN POSSIBLE TO PREVENT THE HARM TO MY CLIENT.

21 YOU CAN EXPECT A MOTION TO COMPEL ANSWERS TO MY QUESTIONS. I KNOW

22 THAT RULE 37 REQUIRES ME TO CERTIFY THAT WE HAVE ATTEMPTED TO SETTLE

23 THE MATTER WITHOUT COURT INTERVENTION. SO I MUST ASK YOU, MA'AM,

24 WHETHER THERE IS ANYTHING THAT WE CAN DO TO INDUCE REV. YUN TO

25 ANSWER MY QUESTIONS OR ANY WAY WE CAN GET THIS INFORMATION BY OTHER

26 MEANS.

27   MS. RUMSDALE: NOTHING I CAN THINK OF. REV. YUN INTENDS TO STAND

[Document page 15]

1   ON HER PRIVILEGE AND NOT TO TESTIFY ABOUT CONFIDENTIAL

2   COMMUNICATIONS FROM ANYONE WHO HAS SOUGHT HER OUT IN HER CAPACITY AS

3   A MINISTER.

4   MR. DUPRIEST: WELL, SUBJECT TO REOPENING IN THE EVENT JUDGE

5   DRAFTER DISAGREES WITH YOU, I GUESS WE ARE THROUGH HERE. REV. YUN,

6   LET ME JUST ASK YOU TO GO OVER IN YOUR MIND THE TESTIMONY YOU HAVE

7   GIVEN HERE THIS MORNING AND I ASK WHETHER ANY OF YOUR ANSWERS MAY

8   NOT HAVE BEEN EXACTLY WHAT YOU MEANT TO SAY OR WHETHER THERE IS

9   ANYTHING YOU NEED TO ADD TO YOUR PREVIOUS TESTIMONY IN ORDER TO FILL

10 ANY GAPS OR CLARIFY YOUR TESTIMONY. IS THERE ANYTHING YOU WANT TO

11 ADD AT THIS POINT IN TIME?

12   THE WITNESS: THANK YOU. YOU ARE VERY COURTEOUS, BUT I REALLY

13 DON'T HAVE ANYTHING TO ADD. YOU WERE VERY THOROUGH.

14   MR. DUPRIEST: WELL, WE APPRECIATE YOUR COMING DOWN TODAY. THIS

15 DEPOSITION IS CONCLUDED.

16   THE REPORTER: USUAL STIPULATIONS?

17   MR. DUPRIEST: CERTAINLY.

18   MS. RUMSDALE: YES.

19   (AT 11:24 A.M., MARCH 30, YR-00, THE DEPOSITION OF HARRIETT YUN

20 WAS ADJOURNED.)

21 //

22 //

23 //

24 /

25 //

26 //

27 //

1   <u>REPORTER'S CERTIFICATE</u>

2   I, LEONARD AHERN, OFFICIAL COURT REPORTER OF THE STATE OF

3 ALABAMA, HEREBY CERTIFY THAT THE FOREGOING DEPOSITION OF HARRIETT

4 YUN WAS TAKEN BEFORE ME AT THE TIME AND PLACE HEREIN SET FORTH, AT

5 WHICH TIME THE WITNESS WAS PUT ON OATH BY ME;

6   THAT THE TESTIMONY OF THE WITNESS AND ALL OBJECTIONS MADE AT THE

7 TIME OF EXAMINATION WERE RECORDED STENOGRAPHICALLY BY ME, AND WERE

8 THEREAFTER TRANSCRIBED UNDER MY DIRECT SUPERVISION.

9   I FURTHER CERTIFY THAT I AM NEITHER COUNSEL FOR NOR RELATED TO

10 ANY PARTY TO SAID ACTION, NOR AM I IN ANYWISE INTERESTED IN THE

11 OUTCOME THEREOF.

12   IN WITNESS WHEREOF, I HAVE SUBSCRIBED MY NAME ON APRIL 2, YR-00.

Leonard Ahern

Armand DuPriest
Wilson & DuPriest
900 Maple Lane
Bald Mountain, Alabama 36918
Telephone: (934) 444-2541

UNITED STATES DISTRICT COURT
FILED
April 5, YR-00
WESTERN DISTRICT OF ALABAMA

In the
United States District Court
for the Western District of Alabama

Ernestine Petrillo,	)	
	)	
Plaintiff	)	Civil Action No. 00-85FD
v.	)	
	)	
Linwood Rooks,	)	
Harriett Yun, and	)	
Bald Mountain Community Church,	)	
	)	
Defendants	)	

PLAINTIFF'S MOTION TO COMPEL
DEFENDANT YUN TO ANSWER DEPOSITION QUESTIONS

Plaintiff, Ernestine Petrillo, through her undersigned counsel, hereby moves the court

pursuant to Fed. R. Civ. P. 37(a)(2), for an order directing the defendant Harriett Yun to

answer certain questions propounded to her in her deposition taken on March 30, YR-00.

The particular questions that the deponent refused to answer are set forth in excerpts from

the transcript attached hereto as Exhibit B. This motion is based on the grounds that the

deponent failed without justification to answer the questions, as is more fully set forth in

the declarations of Armand DuPriest and Esther Borzoi, attached hereto as Exhibits A and

C.

Undersigned counsel certifies that he has in good faith conferred with the deponent,

through her counsel, Emily Rumsdale, Esquire, in an unsuccessful effort to secure the

information without court action.

Respectfully submitted,

Dated: April 4, YR-00   *Armand DuPriest*

Armand DuPriest

Wilson & DuPriest
900 Maple Lane
Bald Mountain, Alabama 36918
Telephone: (934) 444-2541

Attorney for the Plaintiff
Ernestine Petrillo

PROOF OF SERVICE

I certify that on this 4th day of April, YR-00, I served the foregoing Motion to Compel the Defendant Yun to Answer Deposition Questions, and Exhibits A, B, and C attached thereto, upon the defendants by causing a copy thereof to be delivered by hand to counsel for the defendants, Emily Rumsdale, Esquire, Miller, Eldridge & Pasternak, 13304 Bald Mountain Parkway, Bald Mountain, Alabama 36918.

Armand DuPriest

Armand DuPriest

Wilson & DuPriest
900 Maple Lane
Bald Mountain, Alabama 36918
Telephone: (934) 444-2541

Attorney for the Plaintiff
Ernestine Petrillo

EXHIBIT A

DECLARATION OF ARMAND DUPRIEST

I, Armand DuPriest, hereby declare under penalty of perjury:

1. I am the attorney of record for the plaintiff in this action, Ernestine Petrillo.

2. On March 30, YR-00, I took the deposition of Harriett Yun, one of the defendants in this action. The transcript of this deposition was filed on April 2, YR-00. The deposition was taken in compliance with this court's Scheduling Order dated January 29, YR-00.

3. During the course of the deposition, I asked, and the deponent refused to answer, several questions concerning a prior conversation between the deponent and Esther Borzoi. The particular questions are set forth in an excerpt from the transcript of the said deposition, attached hereto as Exhibit B.

4. The grounds assigned by the deponent and her counsel for the deponent's refusal to answer the questions was Alabama Evidence Rule 505, Confidential Communications to Clergy.

5. The communication between Esther Borzoi and the deponent was not confidential and was not communicated to the deponent in her professional capacity as a member of the clergy. If the communication was confidential, that confidentiality has been expressly waived, as set forth in the declaration of Esther Borzoi, attached hereto as Exhibit C.

Dated: April 4, YR-00   *Armand DuPriest*

                                         Armand DuPriest

EXHIBIT B

EXCERPTS FROM TRANSCRIPT OF DEPOSITION OF HARRIETT YUN

Q   Have you had conversations with Esther Borzoi?

A   Yes.

Q   Did you have a conversation with her in December YR-03, approximately in the second week of December?

A   Yes.

Q   What did you discuss?

A   I am not at liberty to say. [Tr. 41, lines 1-7.]

* * *

Q   Isn't it true that what she told you she had learned in her capacity as an employee and she was afraid of getting in trouble in connection with her work?

A   I am not at liberty to say.

Q   Isn't it true that Esther Borzoi told you that she had heard from at least two people who were clients in pastoral counseling of Rev. Rooks that Mr. Rooks was urging them to invest in a bed and breakfast business that he was starting up? [Tr. 41, line 21 - Tr. 42, line 1.]

* * *

Q   I also intended to ask you whether Ms. Borzoi had mentioned to you a conversation that she had with Rev. Rooks on the subject of his bed and breakfast business and another conversation that she had with an assistant pastor, who told Ms. Borzoi that he had heard complaints about Mr. Rooks' mixing personal business with counseling. Would I be correct in assuming that you would refuse to answer those questions for the same reasons?

A   Yes. [Tr. 42, lines 12-19.]

* * *

Q   Knowing that Ms. Borzoi no longer wishes that conversation to be kept secret, would you now be willing to answer my previous questions about your conversation with her in December YR-03?

A   No. * * * [Tr. 43 lines 3-6.]

EXHIBIT C

DECLARATION OF ESTHER BORZOI

I, Esther Borzoi, hereby declare under penalty of perjury:

1. I have been a member of Bald Mountain Community Church since YR-07. Off
    and on from about June YR-03 until the present, I have worked part-time in the
    church office. I estimate that I average approximately six hours per week, for
    which I am paid minimum wage.

2. I am acquainted with the defendant, Rev. Harriett Yun, the church's senior
    pastor. I have often confided in her about matters of personal and spiritual
    concern. I am also acquainted with the defendant, Rev. Linwood Rooks, who
    was until his resignation on July 1, YR-01, the church's associate pastor in charge
    of pastoral counseling.

3. In early November YR-03, I began hearing rumors that Rev. Rooks was involved
    in a business to promote religiously oriented bed and breakfast inns, and that he
    was soliciting investments from members of the congregation. This seemed
    peculiar to me, but I did not think much about it.

4. A couple of weeks later, in mid- to late-November, I conversed separately with
    two friends of mine who are members of the congregation and who told me they
    were pastoral counseling clients of Rev. Rooks. Each of my friends recounted
    that Rev. Rooks had been pressuring them to invest in his bed and breakfast
    business. He told each of them that it would be both spiritually and financially

[Document page 6]

beneficial. My friends said that they tried to change the subject whenever Rev. Rooks would bring up the idea of their investing, but he became very persistent and adamant. One of my friends quit counseling because of the pressure she felt. The other said she made a small investment, but that did not stop Rev. Rooks from pressuring her for more investment. I also talked with an assistant pastor, who told me he had heard complaints about Rev. Rooks mixing personal business with pastoral counseling.

5. I felt sorry for my friends being put in this position. It did not seem right to me that a pastoral counselor should be pressuring people to invest in a business in which he had a personal financial stake. However, I did not tell anyone because I did not want to make Rev. Rooks mad. I brooded about this, because one of my worst character flaws is that I often hesitate to do what I know is the right thing because I am afraid I will make someone mad.

6. I fretted about this for a couple of weeks and then decided I needed to tell someone. Sometime in the second week of December YR-03, I went to see Rev. Yun in her office. I told her that I wanted to speak to her in confidence about a matter that was worrying me. She said all right, invited me in, and closed the door. No one else was present for this conversation. I told Rev. Yun about the things I had heard about Rev. Rooks, as set forth in paragraphs 3 and 4, above. I also told her about my feelings, as set forth in paragraph 5 above. Rev. Yun talked with me about the temptations that pastors sometimes face and about how

[Document page 7]

all members of a church community should feel good about supporting all other members, including their pastors. She congratulated me for being willing to speak up in spite of my fear. And she said she would look into Rev. Rooks' conduct and see if there was anything that she, as senior pastor, should do.

7. I had several reasons for approaching Rev. Yun. As a church member, I was worried that one of the pastors seemed to be doing something wrong, and I hoped Rev. Yun would look into this and put a stop to it.. As an employee of the church, I was afraid that I might get in trouble if Rev. Yun found out that I had such important information and did not do anything about it. As a "work in progress" type of human being, I valued Rev. Yun's mature perspective and warm demeanor to help me get over my excessive fear of making people mad at me.

8. After the scandal about Rev. Rooks came out and when I found out about what he had done to Ernestine Petrillo, I decided that I no longer wanted to keep my information secret. The information is important to help right some of the wrongs that Rev. Rooks inflicted on innocent people. I want to tell the story not only of what I heard, but also the story of how I went to Rev. Yun and told her about it, but it didn't seem to do any good.

9. On August 26,YR-01, I spoke with Rev. Yun and told her that I no longer wanted to keep our conversation of December YR-03 a secret and that I desired to release her from any obligation of confidentiality.

[Document page 8]

10. I hereby waive and release any privilege of confidentiality that I may have in the fact and contents of my conversation with Rev. Yun in December YR-03, as described above.

Dated: April 3, YR-00

Esther Borzoi

Emily Rumsdale
Miller, Eldridge & Pasternak
13304 Bald Mountain Parkway
Bald Mountain, Alabama 36918
Telephone (934) 485-9000

```
┌─────────────────────────────────────┐
│ UNITED STATES DISTRICT COURT         │
│          FILED                       │
│    April 10, YR-00                   │
│ WESTERN DISTRICT OF ALABAMA          │
└─────────────────────────────────────┘
```

Attorney for Defendants
Rev. Harriett Yun and
Bald Mountain Community Church

In the
United States District Court
for the Western District of Alabama

Ernestine Petrillo,)	
)	
Plaintiff)	
v.)	Civil Action No. 00-85FD
)	
Linwood Rooks, et al.)	
)	
Defendants)	

DEFENDANTS' MOTION TO STRIKE EXHIBIT C
OF PLAINTIFF'S MOTION TO COMPEL

The defendants Rev. Harriett Yun and Bald Mountain Community Church

hereby move to strike Exhibit C to Plaintiff's Motion to Compel Defendant Yun to

Answer Deposition Questions and request that Exhibit C be suppressed as

evidence in this case.

[Document page 1]

Rev. Yun's testimony on deposition establishes that her conversation with

Esther Borzoi in December YR-03 was a confidential communication from Ms.

Borzoi to Rev. Yun in her professional capacity as a member of the clergy and is

therefore privileged under Alabama Rule of Evidence 505. The clergy member

may claim the privilege in her own right, Rule 505(c), and is entitled "to prevent

another from disclosing the confidential communication," Rule 505(b). The

communicating person cannot waive the clergy person's separate and

independent privilege. Exhibit C to Plaintiff's motion is a blatant attempt to

disclose a confidential communication in violation of Rule 505, and it should be

stricken from the court's records and suppressed as evidence in this case.

Dated: April, 10, YR-00   Respectfully submitted,

                                                 Emily Rumsdale
                                                 _____

                                                 Emily Rumsdale

                                                 Miller, Eldridge & Pasternak
                                                 13304 Bald Mountain Parkway
                                                 Bald Mountain, Alabama 36918
                                                 Telephone (934) 485-9000

                                                 Attorney for Defendants
                                                 Rev. Harriett Yun and
                                                 Bald Mountain Community Church

CERTIFICATE OF SERVICE

I certify that on this 10th day of April, YR-00, I served the foregoing Motion to Strike Exhibit C of Plaintiff's Motion to Compel Defendant Yun to Answer Deposition Questions by causing a copy thereof to be hand-delivered to the attorney for the plaintiff, Armand DuPriest, at Wilson & DuPriest, 900 Maple Lane, Bald Mountain, Alabama 36918.

Emily Rumsdale

Emily Rumsdale

Miller, Eldridge & Pasternak
13304 Bald Mountain Parkway
Bald Mountain, Alabama 36918
Telephone (934) 485-9000

Attorney for Defendants
Rev. Harriett Yun and
Bald Mountain Community Church

IN THE UNITED STATES DISTRICT COURT
FOR THE WESTERN DISTRICT OF ALABAMA

ERNESTINE PETRILLO   :

    PLAINTIFF   :

VS.   :

LINWOOD ROOKS, ET AL.   :

    DEFENDANTS   :

                            :

```
┌─────────────────────────────────────┐
│      UNITED STATES DISTRICT COURT    │
│              FILED                   │
│        April 14, YR-00               │
│      WESTERN DISTRICT OF ALABAMA     │
└─────────────────────────────────────┘
```

CIVIL ACTION NO. 00-85FD

DEPOSITION OF ERNESTINE PETRILLO

TAKEN BY DEFENDANTS AT 13304 BALD MOUNTAIN PARKWAY, BALD MOUNTAIN,
ALABAMA, COMMENCING AT 1:30 P.M., APRIL 7, YR-00,
BEFORE LEONARD AHERN, OFFICIAL COURT REPORTER

APPEARANCES:

    FOR DEFENDANTS HARRIETT YUN AND BALD MOUNTAIN COMMUNITY CHURCH:

        MILLER, ELDRIDGE & PASTERNAK

            BY: EMILY RUMSDALE, ESQ.

        13304 BALD MOUNTAIN PARKWAY
        BALD MOUNTAIN, ALABAMA 36918
        TELEPHONE (934) 485-9000

    FOR PLAINTIFF:

        WILSON & DUPRIEST

            BY: ARMAND DUPRIEST, ESQ.

        900 MAPLE LANE
        BALD MOUNTAIN, ALABAMA 36918
        TELEPHONE (934) 333-2541

[Document page 1]

1   BALD MOUNTAIN, ALABAMA, APRIL 7, YR-00

2   ERNESTINE PETRILLO

3   HAVING BEEN DULY SWORN, TESTIFIED AS FOLLOWS:

4   EXAMINATION ON BEHALF OF THE DEFENDANTS

5   MS. RUMSDALE:

6   GOOD MORNING. ON THE RECORD IN CIVIL ACTION NO. 00-85. WE ARE

7 HERE FOR THE DEPOSITION OF THE PLAINTIFF ERNESTINE PETRILLO. I AM

8 EMILY RUMSDALE OF THE LAW FIRM OF MILLER, ELDRIDGE & PASTERNAK. I

9 REPRESENT THE DEFENDANTS BALD MOUNTAIN COMMUNITY CHURCH AND THE

10 CHURCH'S SENIOR PASTOR, THE REVEREND HARRIETT YUN. THERE IS ANOTHER

11 DEFENDANT IN THIS ACTION THAT WE DO NOT REPRESENT. THAT'S LINWOOD

12 ROOKS. MR. ROOKS HAS ELECTED NOT TO CONTEST THIS ACTION. HE WAS

13 NOTIFIED OF THIS DEPOSITION BUT EVIDENTLY HE DID NOT CHOOSE TO

14 APPEAR OR BE REPRESENTED IN THESE PROCEEDINGS. JUST TO BE CLEAR,

15 TODAY WHEN I REFER TO THE DEFENDANTS I MEAN SPECIFICALLY THE BALD

16 MOUNTAIN COMMUNITY CHURCH AND REVEREND YUN AND DO NOT INTEND TO

17 REFER TO THE DEFENDANT ROOKS UNLESS I INDICATE OTHERWISE. THE

18 ATTORNEY FOR THE PLAINTIFF IS HERE TODAY. MR. DUPRIEST, WOULD YOU

19 MIND IDENTIFYING YOURSELF FOR THE RECORD?

20   MR. DUPRIEST:

21   NOT AT ALL. THANK YOU. I AM ARMAND DUPRIEST, THAT'S

22 D-U-P-R-I-E-S-T. I REPRESENT THE PLAINTIFF IN THIS ACTION, MS.

23 ERNESTINE PETRILLO.

24   MS. RUMSDALE:

25   IN ADDITION TO MR. DUPRIEST AND MYSELF, WE HAVE PRESENT IN THE

26 ROOM TODAY THE PLAINTIFF, MS. PETRILLO, AND THE COURT REPORTER MR.

27 AHERN.

[Document page 2]

1   BY MS. RUMSDALE:

2   Q   TO BEGIN WITH, MS. PETRILLO, FOR THE RECORD WOULD YOU PLEASE

3   STATE AND SPELL YOUR NAME.

4   A   YES. MY NAME IS ERNESTINE PETRILLO. THAT'S E-R-N-E-S-T-I-N-E

5   P-E-T-R-I-L-L-O.

6   [PRELIMINARY QUESTIONS⁴]

7   * * *

8   Q   YOU ARE THE PLAINTIFF IN THIS ACTION?

9   A   THAT'S CORRECT.

10   Q   AND YOU ARE A MEMBER OF THE DEFENDANT BALD MOUNTAIN COMMUNITY

11   CHURCH, CORRECT?

12   A   I SUPPOSE I AM STILL TECHNICALLY A MEMBER, BUT I NO LONGER

13   LIVE IN BALD MOUNTAIN AND NO LONGER ATTEND THE BALD MOUNTAIN CHURCH.

14   I HAVE A NEW CHURCH HOME IN MADISON, WISCONSIN, WHERE I AM LIVING

15   NOW, BUT I DON'T THINK I EVER TECHNICALLY RESIGNED AS A MEMBER OF

16   BALD MOUNTAIN COMMUNITY CHURCH.

17   Q   WHEN DID YOU MOVE AWAY FROM BALD MOUNTAIN, ALABAMA?

18   A   IN JUNE OF YR-01.

19   Q   AND YOU MOVED DIRECTLY TO MADISON, WISCONSIN?

20   A   YES.

---

[4]It is good practice in taking a deposition to inquire as to the competency of the witness, the witness' understanding of the obligation to testify truthfully, circumstances that might interfere with the witness' ability or willingness to be deposed, and similar matters. These inquiries are designed to inhibit subsequent repudiation of the deposition and to lay the foundation for impeaching the credibility of the witness who testifies inconsistently with the deposition testimony. For the sake of efficiency, it is also good practice to establish ground rules, such as that the witness should answer questions and not volunteer information, should pause and wait for instructions whenever one of the lawyers makes an objection, etc. Rev. Yun's deposition contains an example of such preliminary questions. See pp. 30-33, *supra.* Because matters covered in preliminary questioning are not relevant to the issues raised by this Case File, the preliminary questions are omitted from this and later deposition transcripts. —Ed.]

[Document page 3]

1   Q   WHY DID YOU MOVE?

2   A   PERSONAL AND EDUCATIONAL REASONS.

3   Q   DID YOUR REASONS HAVE ANYTHING TO DO WITH THIS LITIGATION?

4   A   YES AND NO.   I HAD BEEN THINKING ABOUT PURSUING A MASTER'S

5   DEGREE IN LIBRARY SCIENCE. AFTER MY PARENTS' DEATH AND MY BROKEN

6   ENGAGEMENT, I WAS AN EMOTIONAL MESS AND WAS SEEKING A NEW DIRECTION

7   FOR SOME TIME. THEN MY PASTORAL COUNSELING WITH REVEREND ROOKS

8   TURNED INTO A DISASTER. WHEN IT CAME OUT THAT I HAD FOOLISHLY

9   ALLOWED HIM TO SWINDLE ME OUT OF A LOT OF MONEY, I FELT LIKE MY

10 WORLD WAS CRUMBLING AGAIN. THAT'S WHEN I DECIDED IT WAS TIME TO MOVE

11 AWAY FROM THIS TOWN.   MY SISTER IN MADISON ENCOURAGED ME TO COME

12 LIVE WITH HER AND TO LOOK INTO THE MASTERS DEGREE PROGRAM AT THE

13 UNIVERSITY OF WISCONSIN. I DECIDED TO APPLY. FORTUNATELY, I WAS

14 ACCEPTED AND I STARTED THE PROGRAM IN SEPTEMBER. IT TOOK ME BETWEEN

15 JUNE AND SEPTEMBER TO MOVE ALL MY THINGS FROM BALD MOUNTAIN TO

16 MADISON. SO I GUESS YOU COULD SAY THAT THE EVENTS THAT FORCED ME TO

17 BRING THIS LITIGATION WERE PART OF WHAT CAUSED ME TO MOVE TO

18 MADISON, BUT THE LITIGATION ITSELF HAD NOTHING TO DO WITH MY

19 DECISION.

20 Q   WHEN DID YOU FIRST TALK WITH LEGAL COUNSEL ABOUT THE

21 POSSIBILITY OF LITIGATION?

22 A   I CONSULTED WITH LAWYERS - NOT MR. DUPRIEST - SOON AFTER I

23 REALIZED THAT THE MONEY I PUT INTO MR. ROOKS' BUSINESS WAS PROBABLY

24 A TOTAL LOSS.   MAYBE AROUND APRIL YR-01.

25 Q   AND WERE YOU AWARE THAT BY MOVING TO ANOTHER STATE YOU COULD

26 MAKE IT POSSIBLE TO BRING YOUR LAWSUIT IN A FEDERAL COURT?

27 A   NOT AT THE TIME.   MY LAWYERS DISCUSSED WHETHER WE SHOULD SUE

1   IN STATE OR FEDERAL COURT BUT THAT WAS AFTER I MOVED.

2   MR. DUPRIEST:

3   I OBJECT TO THE LAST QUESTION AND ANSWER AND MOVE TO STRIKE

4   BECAUSE IT VIOLATES MS. PETRILLO'S ATTORNEY-CLIENT PRIVILEGE.

5   MS. RUMSDALE:

6   THAT WAS NOT MY INTENT. YOUR OBJECTION IS IN THE RECORD. IS

7   THERE ANYTHING ELSE YOU NEED?

8   MR. DUPRIEST:

9   WELL I JUST WANT TO POINT OUT TO MS. PETRILLO THAT SHE SHOULD BE

10   CAREFUL NOT TO DISCUSS ANYTHING ABOUT HER COMMUNICATIONS WITH ME OR

11   ANY OTHER LAWYER IN MY FIRM.   AND IF ANYTHING COMES UP THAT YOU ARE

12   NOT SURE ABOUT, YOU SHOULD CONFER WITH ME BEFORE ANSWERING ANY

13   PARTICULAR QUESTION.

14   THE WITNESS:

15   OK, I'LL TRY TO REMEMBER.

16   BY MS. RUMSDALE:

17   Q   WELL, REGARDLESS OF WHERE YOU GOT THE INFORMATION, YOU WERE

18   AWARE WHEN YOU MOVED TO WISCONSIN THAT IT COULD MAKE A BIG

19   DIFFERENCE IN WHERE YOU MIGHT BRING THIS LAW SUIT, RIGHT?

20   A   NO I WASN'T. I DID NOT LEARN ANYTHING ABOUT THAT UNTIL LATER.

21   Q   WHEN DID YOU FIRST START ATTENDING BALD MOUNTAIN COMMUNITY

22   CHURCH?

23   A   MY PARENTS PUT ME IN SUNDAY SCHOOL AND STARTED TAKING ME TO

24   CHURCH WHEN I WAS FIVE OR SIX, AND I AM 24 NOW, SO IT'S ALMOST 20

25   YEARS AGO.

26   Q   WHEN WERE YOU FIRST RECEIVED INTO MEMBERSHIP IN THE CHURCH?

27   A   WHEN I WAS EIGHTEEN. PASTOR YUN DOES NOT BELIEVE THAT

1 CHILDREN SHOULD HAVE FULL MEMBERSHIP, SO WHEN I TURNED EIGHTEEN WAS

2 MY FIRST OPPORTUNITY.

3   Q   WOULD YOU SAY THAT YOU WERE AN ACTIVE MEMBER OF THE CHURCH?

4   A   I WAS ACTIVE IN CHURCH YOUTH ACTIVITIES ALL ALONG. THAT'S

5 WHERE I HAD FRIENDS. I ATTENDED MOST OF THE FELLOWSHIP MEETINGS. I

6 WORKED ON COMMITTEES AND STUFF LIKE THAT. AND WHEN I BECAME A

7 MEMBER, I CONTINUED TO ATTEND CHURCH REGULARLY AND GO TO SUNDAY

8 SCHOOL.

9   Q   DID YOU EVER HAVE ANY LEADERSHIP POSITIONS WITHIN THE CHURCH

10 OR THE YOUTH FELLOWSHIP?

11   A   NOT REALLY. I'M PRETTY SHY AND I DON'T LIKE TO PUT MYSELF OUT

12 THERE. BUT I WAS ELECTED TREASURER OF THE YOUTH FELLOWSHIP IN MY

13 SENIOR YEAR, BUT I WOULDN'T CALL THAT LEADERSHIP, IT WAS JUST TAKING

14 UP THE COLLECTION AND KEEPING TRACK OF THE MONEY.

15   Q   HOW MUCH EDUCATION HAVE YOU HAD?

16   A   I GRADUATED FROM HIGH SCHOOL HERE IN BALD MOUNTAIN AND THEN

17 WENT TO THE UNIVERSITY OF ALABAMA AT BIRMINGHAM WHERE I GOT A B.A.

18 DEGREE IN EDUCATION AND TEACHING CERTIFICATE.

19   Q   WHEN DID YOU GET YOUR DEGREE?

20   A   JUNE YR-03.

21   Q   WHAT DID YOU DO AFTER YOU FINISHED COLLEGE?

22   A   I RETURNED TO BALD MOUNTAIN AND FOUND A JOB TEACHING

23 KINDERGARTEN AT ONE OF THE BALD MOUNTAIN PUBLIC ELEMENTARY SCHOOLS.

24   Q   HOW LONG DID YOU WORK AS A KINDERGARTEN TEACHER?

25   A   FOR TWO YEARS - THROUGH THE END OF THE SCHOOL YEAR IN YR-01.

26   Q   HAVE YOU BEEN EMPLOYED IN ANY OTHER LINE OF WORK?

27   A   I USED TO DO A LOT OF BABY SITTING. AND WHILE I WAS IN

1 COLLEGE I WORKED A COUPLE OF PART-TIME JOBS, ONE IN A CLOTHING STORE

2 AND THE OTHER WORKING AT A DAY CARE.

3 Q ARE YOU EMPLOYED NOW?

4 A NO, I'M A FULL-TIME GRADUATE STUDENT AT THE UNIVERSITY OF

5 WISCONSIN.

6 Q WHEN DID YOU BEGIN YOUR STUDIES AT THE UNIVERSITY OF

7 WISCONSIN?

8 A IT WAS IN SEPTEMBER, YR-01.

9 Q ANY OTHER EMPLOYMENT HISTORY?

10 A NO.

11 Q WHAT ARE YOU STUDYING AT THE UNIVERSITY OF WISCONSIN?

12 A I'M WORKING ON A MASTERS DEGREE IN LIBRARY SCIENCE.

13 Q WHY DID YOU DECIDE TO LEAVE YOUR TEACHING POSITION AND GO

14 BACK TO SCHOOL?

15 A I JUST COULDN'T STAY IN BALD MOUNTAIN ANY MORE – NOT AFTER

16 WHAT HAPPENED WITH MY PARENTS AND WHAT HE – WHAT REVEREND ROOKS HAD

17 DONE. I FELT SO BETRAYED, SO HUMILIATED. I JUST HAD TO GET AWAY.

18 AND I WANTED TO FIND A PEACEFUL LINE OF WORK IN WHICH I WOULDN'T

19 HAVE TO DEAL WITH PEOPLE.

20 Q HOW DID YOU END UP AT THE UNIVERSITY OF WISCONSIN?

21 A WELL, MY OLDER SISTER, MARY, LIVES THERE, AND I HEARD THEY

22 HAD A GOOD PROGRAM. AND IT WAS A LONG WAY FROM BALD MOUNTAIN.

23 Q HOW LONG DOES YOUR DEGREE PROGRAM TAKE THERE?

24 A TWO YEARS.

25 Q ANY PLANS FOR AFTER YOU GRADUATE?

26 A NOTHING SPECIFIC – JUST LOOK FOR A JOB AS A LIBRARIAN.

27 Q WHERE WILL YOU LOOK FOR A JOB?

1   A   MAYBE WISCONSIN. I LIKE IT THERE. IF I CAN'T FIND A JOB

2 THERE, THEN I DON'T KNOW – ANYWHERE BUT ALABAMA.

3   Q   WHAT KIND OF RECREATIONAL ACTIVITIES DO YOU ENGAGE IN?

4   A   NOT MUCH. I READ A LOT OF BOOKS. I WATCH SOME TV. I LIKE TO

5 RIDE MY BIKE. I'VE TAKEN GOURMET COOKING CLASSES AND I GUESS YOU

6 COULD SAY COOKING IS MY HOBBY. OTHER THAN THAT –

7   Q   DO YOU PARTICIPATE IN ANY SPORTS OR FOLLOW ANY SPORTS?

8   A   NO. SPORTS HAVE NEVER INTERESTED ME.

9   Q   HOW ELSE DO YOU FILL YOUR TIME BESIDES YOUR WORK AND THE

10 ACTIVITIES YOU'VE ALREADY MENTIONED?

11   A   THAT'S ABOUT IT. I ENJOY DANCING BUT I DON'T GET ASKED OUT

12 VERY MUCH.

13   Q   WOULD YOU SAY THE SAME PATTERN OF ACTIVITY WAS TRUE WHEN YOU

14 LIVED IN ALABAMA?

15   A   PRETTY MUCH. OF COURSE THERE WERE FAMILY ACTIVITIES, BIRTHDAY

16 PARTIES AND STUFF LIKE THAT. AND WHEN I WAS IN COLLEGE IN

17 BIRMINGHAM I HAD A STEADY BOYFRIEND STARTING IN THE MIDDLE OF MY

18 SENIOR YEAR AND WE WERE STILL DATING AFTER I CAME BACK TO BALD

19 MOUNTAIN. WE USED TO GO DANCING A LOT AND JUST HANGING OUT.

20   Q   IS THAT THE BOYFRIEND WHO BECAME YOUR FIANCÉ, THE ONE YOU

21 WERE ENGAGED TO AND MENTIONED IN YOUR COMPLAINT IN THIS ACTION THAT

22 YOU BROKE UP WITH?

23   A   YES.

24   Q   WHEN WAS YOUR ENGAGEMENT CALLED OFF?

25   A   MAY OF YR-02.

26   Q   DO YOU MIND IF I ASK ABOUT THE CIRCUMSTANCES LEADING TO YOUR

27 ENDING THE ENGAGEMENT?

1   A   I DIDN'T END IT. HE DID. I JUST WAS NOT ENOUGH FOR HIM AFTER

2   MY PARENTS DIED.

3   Q   COULD YOU SAY MORE ABOUT THAT?

4   A   ON DECEMBER 20, YR-03, BOTH OF MY PARENTS WERE KILLED IN A

5   HORRIBLE CAR WRECK. I WAS TOLD ABOUT IT BY A POLICE OFFICER WHO CAME

6   TO THE HOUSE. IT WAS LIKE RIGHT OUT OF THE BLUE I WAS AN ORPHAN. I

7   COULDN'T GET HOLD OF MY BROTHER. THE POLICEMAN MADE ME GO DOWN AND

8   IDENTIFY THEIR BODIES. THEY WERE PRETTY MESSED UP. IT WAS SO GROSS.

9   THE WHOLE THING WAS UNBELIEVABLY TERRIBLE. I WAS VERY CLOSE TO MY

10   PARENTS. THEIR DEATHS DEVASTATED ME. I WAS LIKE A ZOMBIE FOR TWO OR

11   THREE MONTHS. STEVE TRIED TO COMFORT ME BUT I GUESS I JUST COULDN'T

12   BE REACHED AND THAT FRUSTRATED HIM. PRETTY SOON I GUESS HE COULDN'T

13   TAKE MY GRIEVING ANY LONGER AND THAT'S WHEN HE STARTED DATING

14   SOMEONE ELSE BEHIND MY BACK. WELL, ONE THING LED TO ANOTHER AND I

15   TOLD HIM HE WAS GOING TO HAVE TO MAKE A CHOICE, AND HE DID, AND HE

16   CHOSE THE OTHER GIRL, AND THAT WAS IT.

17   Q   SO STEVE, THAT WAS YOUR BOYFRIEND?

18   A   YES, MY FIANCÉ.

19   Q   HE WAS THE ONE WHO TERMINATED YOUR ENGAGEMENT?

20   A   THAT'S RIGHT.

21   Q   AND THAT WAS WHAT PROMPTED YOU TO GO TO PASTORAL COUNSELING?

22   A   WELL, THAT KIND OF OVERSIMPLIFIES IT, BUT YES.

23   Q   WELL, LET ME ASK IT THIS WAY. WOULD YOU PLEASE DESCRIBE THE

24   VARIOUS FACTORS THAT INFLUENCED YOUR DECISION TO SEEK PASTORAL

25   COUNSELING?

26   A   I'VE NEVER BEEN A VERY HAPPY PERSON. AS LONG AS I CAN

27   REMEMBER I'VE WONDERED WHAT WAS WRONG WITH ME. I'VE ALWAYS FELT LIKE

1 I WASN'T GOOD FOR MUCH AND PEOPLE COULD SEE RIGHT THROUGH ME AND SEE

2 WHAT A WORTHLESS PERSON I WAS. STEVE WAS THE FIRST ONE WHO REALLY

3 MADE ME FEEL GOOD. WELL, THAT'S NOT QUITE RIGHT. MY PARENTS, MY

4 DAD ESPECIALLY, HAD A WAY OF PUMPING UP MY CONFIDENCE AND TREATING

5 ME LIKE AN INTERESTING AND VALUABLE PERSON. BUT I DREW BACK FROM MY

6 PARENTS AROUND EIGHTH GRADE AND NOT UNTIL I MET STEVE MY SENIOR YEAR

7 DID I HAVE ANYONE WHO SEEMED TO CARE FOR ME. I GRIEVED TERRIBLY WHEN

8 MY PARENTS DIED AND I WAS REALLY HURT WHEN STEVE LEFT. BUT I FELT I

9 NEEDED COUNSELING FOR MORE THAN JUST GRIEF COUNSELING. I WAS

10 DOUBTING WHETHER I WAS WORTH ANYTHING. I GUESS I FELT LIKE THAT IF

11 I WAS ANY GOOD MY PARENTS AND MY FIANCÉ WOULD NOT HAVE ABANDONED ME.

12 I HAD ALWAYS BELIEVED IN A LOVING GOD. NOW I WAS BEGINNING TO WONDER

13 ABOUT THAT. IF GOD LOVES ME SO MUCH, HOW COME HE WAS SENDING SUCH

14 HORRIBLE STUFF INTO MY LIFE? SO I WANTED COUNSELING TO HELP ME WITH

15 SELF-ESTEEM ISSUES AND I WANTED RELIGIOUS COUNSELING TO HELP ME

16 PATCH UP MY RELATIONSHIP WITH GOD.

17   Q   DID YOU FIND ANSWERS?

18   A   TO WHAT?

19   Q   YOUR QUESTION ABOUT HOW A LOVING GOD COULD SEND SUCH HORRIBLE

20 STUFF INTO YOUR LIFE.

21   A   WELL I GUESS SO. I CAME TO REALIZE THAT GOD'S PURPOSES ARE

22 JUST TOO GRAND FOR US HIS TINY CREATURES TO UNDERSTAND.

23   Q   BEFORE YOU WENT INTO COUNSELING WITH REVEREND ROOKS, HAD YOU

24 EVER BEFORE HAD ANY COUNSELING OF ANY SORT OR ANY PSYCHOTHERAPY OR

25 HAD YOU EVER BEEN SEEN BY A PSYCHIATRIST?

26   A   NO, I —

27   Q   HOW DID YOU —

[Document page 10]

1   A I HAD HIGH SCHOOL GUIDANCE COUNSELING TO HELP ME PLAN FOR MY

2 EDUCATION AND WHAT CAREER I WANTED TO GO INTO, BUT THAT'S NOT QUITE

3 THE SAME. THAT DOES NOT GO VERY DEEPLY INTO PERSONAL ISSUES.

4   Q ONCE YOU DECIDED THAT YOU NEEDED SOME SORT OF HELP, WHY DID

5 YOU DECIDE ON REVEREND ROOKS?

6   A HE WAS THE ONLY ONE I THOUGHT OF. HE HAD ARRIVED AT OUR

7 CHURCH ABOUT SIX MONTHS EARLIER WITH GREAT FANFARE HOW HE WAS GOING

8 TO RUN THIS WONDERFUL PASTORAL COUNSELING CENTER. I AND A LOT OF

9 OTHER FEMALES IN THE CONGREGATION WERE ATTRACTED TO HIM. HE WAS

10 HANDSOME AND A GOOD DRESSER AND HE HAD A TWINKLE IN HIS EYE. I

11 DON'T KNOW, I MAYBE WANTED TO GO INTO COUNSELING JUST TO GET TO KNOW

12 HIM BETTER, BUT THAT'S NOT REALLY TRUE. BUT AS SOON AS I THOUGHT

13 ABOUT PASTORAL COUNSELING REVEREND ROOKS WAS THE ONLY ONE WHO

14 ENTERED MY MIND.

15   Q HOW DID YOU GO ABOUT ARRANGING TO SEE REVEREND ROOKS?

16   A SIMPLE, I CALLED HIS OFFICE AND ASKED FOR AN APPOINTMENT, AND

17 HE GAVE ME AN APPOINTMENT THE NEXT DAY.

18   Q WHEN WAS THAT?

19   A WELL, IT WAS ABOUT TEN DAYS OR SO AFTER STEVE TOLD ME THE

20 ENGAGEMENT WAS OFF, I DON'T KNOW THE EXACT DATE. SOMETIME IN THE

21 MIDDLE OF MAY OF YR-02.

22   Q WHAT WAS PASTORAL COUNSELING LIKE FOR YOU?

23   A AT FIRST IT WAS VERY COMFORTING. REVEREND ROOKS WAS A

24 WONDERFUL LISTENER. HE TOOK ME SERIOUSLY AND THAT MADE ME FEEL

25 IMPORTANT. HE COULD COME UP WITH THE MOST AMAZING BIBLE PASSAGES FOR

26 ME TO TAKE HOME AND READ, AND THEY WOULD SPEAK DIRECTLY TO WHATEVER

27 I WAS WORRIED ABOUT. BUT AFTER A WHILE REVEREND ROOKS STOPPED BEING

1   QUITE SO SUPPORTIVE AND HE BECAME A LITTLE CONFRONTATIONAL.

2   Q   WHAT DO YOU MEAN? COULD YOU GIVE AN EXAMPLE?

3   A   WELL, ONE TIME I WAS TALKING ABOUT A RUN-IN I HAD WITH THE

4   PRINCIPAL AT THE SCHOOL WHERE I TAUGHT, MS. WENTWORTH. MS.

5   WENTWORTH THOUGHT I HAD MESSED UP THE PLANS FOR A SCHOOL ASSEMBLY

6   THAT THE PARENTS WERE INVITED TO. AND REALLY IT WAS THE PRINCIPAL

7   WHO HAD MESSED IT UP BY TRYING TO REARRANGE THE SCHEDULE HERSELF AND

8   NOT TELLING ME ABOUT IT. AND I WAS REALLY ANGRY ABOUT THAT BUT I

9   FELT THERE WAS NO WAY I COULD CONFRONT HER WITHOUT GETTING FIRED

10   FROM MY JOB. REVEREND ROOKS TOLD ME MY FEAR WAS IRRATIONAL AND I

11   SHOULD STAND UP TO MS. WENTWORTH AND NOT PUT UP WITH BEING ABUSED

12   WHEN I WAS JUST DOING MY JOB. WE DID A COUPLE OF ROLE PLAYS AND HE

13   WAS PUSHING ME TO SAY THINGS I WOULDN'T DREAM OF SAYING BUT HE KEPT

14   PUSHING AND PUSHING AND FINALLY I REALIZED I COULD DO IT IF I WANTED

15   AND MS. WENTWORTH WASN'T GOING TO FIRE ME. I WAS TOO GOOD WITH THE

16   KINDERGARTEN KIDS. AND SHE WASN'T GOING TO KILL ME, WHICH IT FELT

17   LIKE AT FIRST. I REALIZED THAT SHE MIGHT ACTUALLY RESPECT ME FOR

18   SPEAKING UP FOR MYSELF, AND THAT'S JUST HOW IT WORKED OUT. SO THEN

19   REVEREND ROOKS STARTED TO PICK ON ME ABOUT OTHER THINGS I WOULD DO

20   OR NOT DO BECAUSE OF MY FEARS. LIKE BEING WILLING TO RETURN CLOTHES

21   I BOUGHT BUT DIDN'T LIKE. LIKE NOT LETTING MY GIRLFRIENDS WALK ALL

22   OVER ME. LIKE THE WAY I DRESSED.

23   Q   WHAT ABOUT THE WAY YOU DRESSED?

24   A   WELL, I'VE ALWAYS BEEN A CONSERVATIVE DRESSER, JUST LIKE MY

25   MOM. THEN ONE DAY I WAS TALKING ABOUT BUYING SOME CLOTHES AND

26   REVEREND ROOKS ASKED IF I WAS GOING TO JUST BUY MORE OF THE SAME OLD

27   DOWDY CLOTHES I ALWAYS WORE. I WAS SHOCKED. AND HE CONTINUED TO

[handwritten margin note: Speak up for herself]

[Document page 12]

1   INSULT THE WAY I DRESSED. BUT AFTER A WHILE I REALIZED HE WAS

2   RIGHT. HE SAID SOME PRETTY UNCOMPLIMENTARY THINGS ABOUT HOW I

3   DRESSED, BUT AT THE SAME TIME HE WAS VERY FLATTERING ABOUT HOW

4   ATTRACTIVE I WAS AND HOW I WOULD BE SO MUCH HAPPIER AND SELF-

5   ACCEPTING IF I WOULD JUST DRESS MORE STYLISHLY, AND HOW I COULD PULL

6   IT OFF EVEN THOUGH I WAS SCARED AT FIRST. SO I WENT OUT AND BOUGHT

7   A COUPLE OF CUTE OUTFITS THAT WERE PRETTY DARING COMPARED TO THE

8   CLOTHES I USUALLY WORE. THEY WERE SORT OF SEXY, AND THE FIRST TIME I

9   WENT OUT WITH MY GIRLFRIEND TO A SINGLES PLACE DRESSED LIKE THAT

10   SUDDENLY GUYS WERE HITTING ON ME, NOT IN AN OBNOXIOUS WAY BUT A

11   REALLY NICE WAY, AND IT MADE ME FEEL SO ATTRACTIVE. I COMPLETELY

12   CHANGED MY LOOK IN CLOTHING. I STARTED TO WEAR MAKE-UP. I BOUGHT A

13   VERY CLASSY, PROFESSIONAL WARDROBE AND REALLY SHARP CASUAL CLOTHING,

14   AND I FELT SO MUCH BETTER THAT I COULD ALWAYS FIND THE RIGHT THING

15   TO WEAR TO ANY OCCASION AND I DON'T FEEL DOWDY ANY MORE. AND I WAS

16   OK ABOUT DRESSING KINDA SEXY WHEN I FEEL LIKE IT. NONE OF THAT

17   WOULD HAVE HAPPENED IF REVEREND ROOKS HAD NOT CONFRONTED ME.

18   Q   WHEN DID REVEREND ROOKS FIRST TALK TO YOU ABOUT HIS BED AND

19   BREAKFAST BUSINESS?

20   A   HE WAS VERY OPEN ABOUT HIS OWN LIFE. HE OFTEN USED EXAMPLES

21   FROM HIS OWN LIFE TO ILLUSTRATE THINGS HE WAS SAYING ABOUT HOW

22   PEOPLE FEEL AND BEHAVE AND HOW THEIR FEELINGS CAN GET IN THE WAY OF

23   HOW THEY WANT TO ACT. AND ALSO, WE WOULD SPEND A FEW MINUTES OF EACH

24   SESSION JUST SORT OF SOCIALIZING. LIKE WHAT DID YOU DO THIS WEEKEND?

25   I SAW A GOOD MOVIE. HE WENT WHITE WATER RAFTING, STUFF LIKE THAT. SO

26   I KNEW PRETTY MUCH FROM THE BEGINNING THAT HE AND A BUSINESS

27   PARTNER, ANOTHER MINISTER, HAD THIS BUSINESS THAT THEY WERE TRYING

[Document page 13]

1 TO GET STARTED. IT SOUNDED PRETTY WEIRD AT FIRST, BUT HE LIKED TO

2 TALK ABOUT IT AND AFTER A WHILE IT STARTED TO MAKE SENSE.

3   Q   WHAT DID HE TELL YOU ABOUT THE BUSINESS?

4   A   WELL THE BASIC IDEA WAS THAT THERE ARE A LOT OF PEOPLE WHO

5 LIKE TO TAKE TIME OFF TO NURTURE THEIR SPIRITUAL LIVES AND A LOT OF

6 PEOPLE WHO LIKE TO GO ON MINI VACATIONS, BUT MOST PEOPLE DON'T HAVE

7 TIME FOR ALL THE THINGS THEY WANT TO DO. SO HIS IDEA WAS TO CREATE A

8 SETTING IN WHICH PEOPLE FOCUS ON THEIR SPIRITUAL LIFE AND ALSO ENJOY

9 THE RELAXATION AND RECREATION OF A VACATION. AND THEY WOULD USE THE

10 BED AND BREAKFAST INN MODEL WHICH SO MANY PEOPLE LIKE BETTER THAN A

11 REGULAR HOTEL OR MOTEL AND WHICH ALSO WOULD ALLOW THEM TO GET

12 STARTED ON A SMALL SCALE AND OPERATE ON A SMALLER BUDGET.

13   Q   SO THAT WAS THE IDEA. WHAT DID HE TELL YOU ABOUT THE

14 UNFOLDING OF THAT IDEA, HOW THE BUSINESS WAS GOING, AND THE LIKE?

15   A   WELL HE TALKED ABOUT HOW HE AND HIS PARTNER WERE GETTING

16 INVESTORS AND WHEN THEY HAD ENOUGH CAPITAL THEY COULD QUALIFY FOR A

17 LOAN TO REALLY GET THE BUSINESS GOING. THEN ONE TIME HE TOLD HOW

18 THEY HAD QUALIFIED FOR THE LOAN AND WERE PUTTING BIDS ON SEVERAL

19 PROPERTIES. THEY WERE ALSO RECRUITING MINISTERS AND OTHER PEOPLE OF

20 THE SPIRIT TO HELP PLAN AND THEN OPERATE THESE PROPERTIES. WHEN HE

21 TOLD ME THE FIRST INN HAD OPENED HE SEEMED REALLY EXCITED AND WANTED

22 TO TELL ME ALL ABOUT IT.

23   Q   DID ALL OF THIS TALK ABOUT HIS BUSINESS ENTERPRISE SEEM

24 APPROPRIATE TO YOU?

25   A   WHY NOT? I HAD NEVER BEEN IN COUNSELING BEFORE SO I DID NOT

26 KNOW WHAT TO EXPECT. IT WAS JUST LIKE CONVERSATION, AND I DIDN'T SEE

27 ANYTHING WRONG WITH THAT. IT'S NOT LIKE WE SPENT WHOLE SESSIONS

[Document page 14]

1   TALKING ABOUT HIS BUSINESS. IT DIDN'T GET IN THE WAY OF TALKING

2   ABOUT THE THINGS THAT I WAS IN COUNSELING FOR.

3   Q   ACCORDING TO YOUR COMPLAINT THERE CAME A TIME WHEN YOU MADE A

4   SUBSTANTIAL INVESTMENT IN REVEREND ROOKS' BUSINESS, IS THAT RIGHT?

5   A   WELL, YES. ACTUALLY I MADE TWO INVESTMENTS. THE FIRST WAS A

6   FEW THOUSAND AND THEN OVER A HUNDRED THOUSAND.

7   Q   IS THAT BECAUSE REVEREND ROOKS' DESCRIPTION OF THE BUSINESS

8   GOT YOU INTERESTED IN INVESTING IN IT?

9   A   NOT REALLY. I HAD NO INTEREST IN INVESTING IN ANYTHING LIKE

10 THAT. I THOUGHT HE HAD AN INTERESTING IDEA AND I ENJOYED HEARING

11 ABOUT THEIR EFFORTS TO GET IT OFF THE GROUND BUT I NEVER THOUGHT OF

12 IT AS AN INVESTMENT OPPORTUNITY UNTIL MR. ROOKS BROUGHT IT UP.

13   Q   WHEN DID HE FIRST BRING UP THE IDEA OF YOUR INVESTING IN HIS

14 B AND B BUSINESS? WHAT DID HE SAY?

15   A   I HAD BEEN IN COUNSELING APPROXIMATELY THREE MONTHS. IT WAS

16 SOME TIME IN AUGUST OF YR-02. AND IT CAME UP SORT OF THE SAME WAY AS

17 DOWDY CLOTHES.

18   Q   WHAT DO YOU MEAN?

19   A   MY PARENTS WERE PRETTY WELL FIXED. AFTER THEY DIED, I FOUND

20 OUT THAT I WAS GOING TO INHERIT OVER A MILLION DOLLARS. THEY HAD A

21 LOT OF THEIR MONEY AND DAD'S RETIREMENT FUNDS INVESTED IN EQUITIES,

22 WHICH I THOUGHT WAS PRETTY RISKY. SO AS SOON AS THEIR INVESTMENTS

23 WERE PAID OVER TO ME BY THE EXECUTOR, I STARTED SELLING OFF THE

24 EQUITIES AND INVESTING IN CD'S AND GOVERNMENT BONDS. WHEN I TOLD

25 REVEREND ROOKS ABOUT THIS, HE WAS FLABBERGASTED. HE SAID THAT AT MY

26 AGE I COULD TAKE A MUCH MORE AGGRESSIVE STANCE. BUT THIS WAS NOT

27 JUST FINANCIAL ADVICE. IT WAS ABOUT ME AND MY VALUES AND MY HANG-

[Document page 15]

1 UPS. I WAS REALLY SCARED TO FOLLOW ANYTHING OTHER THAN AN EXTREMELY

2 SAFE AND CONSERVATIVE INVESTMENT STRATEGY. I HAD NO CONFIDENCE IN MY

3 ABILITY TO KNOW THE DIFFERENCE BETWEEN A GOOD INVESTMENT AND A BAD

4 ONE. I WAS SURE THAT THE MOMENT I PUT ANYTHING INTO THE STOCK MARKET

5 THE MARKET WOULD CRASH AND I WOULD BE WIPED OUT. BUT IT WAS WORSE

6 THAN THAT. I DID NOT THINK I DESERVED TO HAVE MUCH MONEY, MUCH LESS

7 BE WEALTHY AND A SUCCESSFUL INVESTOR. SO MY INVESTMENTS WERE DOWDY

8 JUST LIKE MY CLOTHES. AND HE BEGAN TO ENCOURAGE ME TO TAKE SOME

9 SMALL STEPS THAT WOULD BE A BIT MORE ADVENTUROUS. HE ALSO

10 ENCOURAGED ME TO BELIEVE THAT IT WOULD BE OK TO ACTUALLY INVEST IN A

11 REAL BUSINESS AS OPPOSED TO STOCKS IN A HUGE COMPANY OR MUTUAL

12 FUNDS. THAT'S WHEN HE STARTED SUGGESTING THAT HIS B AND B BUSINESS

13 WOULD BE AN IDEAL INVESTMENT FOR ME. I KNEW A LOT ABOUT THE

14 BUSINESS BASED ON OUR CONVERSATIONS. I HAD BECOME QUITE INTERESTED

15 IN THE WHOLE IDEA. AND ALTHOUGH I DID NOT THINK IT WOULD BE A GET

16 RICH SCHEME, I EXPECTED THAT IN THE LONG RUN IT COULD BE A GOOD

17 INVESTMENT.

18   Q   EXACTLY WHAT WERE THE CIRCUMSTANCES WHEN YOU MADE YOUR FIRST

19 INVESTMENT IN THE B AND B BUSINESS?

20   A   IT WAS A COUPLE OF MONTHS AFTER WE GOT ONTO THE ISSUE OF MY

21 FEARS AND INSECURITIES AROUND MONEY. HE HAD ALREADY CRITICIZED THE

22 WAY I DRESSED. HE HAD ENCOURAGED ME TO DO SOMETHING THAT WOULD FEEL

23 A BIT DARING. THAT'S WHEN I WENT OUT AND BOUGHT THE SEXY LITTLE

24 COCKTAIL DRESS THAT I MENTIONED EARLIER AND HAD SUCH A GOOD TIME. SO

25 I MENTIONED HOW GREAT THAT FELT THE NEXT TIME I SAW REVEREND ROOKS.

26 AND HE SAID HE WONDERED WHETHER SOMETHING SMALL BUT EQUALLY DARING

27 AROUND MONEY AND INVESTMENTS WOULD HAVE THE SAME EFFECT. HE ASKED ME

[Document page 16]

1　IF I HAD THOUGHT ABOUT PUTTING A LITTLE BIT INTO THE B AND B

2　BUSINESS, AND THAT'S WHEN HE GAVE ME REVEREND BURR'S NUMBER TO FIND

3　OUT ABOUT THE DETAILS.　I CALLED MS. BURR AND LEARNED THE BUSINESS

4　WAS A LIMITED PARTNERSHIP AND THAT SHARES WERE SELLING FOR TWO

5　THOUSAND DOLLARS EACH.　AND I WAS FEELING SO GIDDY AND OPTIMISTIC

6　FOLLOWING THE TRIUMPH OF THAT FIRST CUTE OUTFIT AND I WAS FEELING SO

7　COMPETENT TALKING WITH A BUSINESS WOMAN AND DRESSED IN MY FIRST REAL

8　BUSINESS SUIT THAT I JUST SAID THE HELL WITH IT AND ASKED HER TO

9　SELL ME TWO SHARES, AND SO THAT'S HOW I CAME TO INVEST THE FIRST

10　FOUR THOUSAND.

11　　Q　IT SOUNDS AS IF REVEREND ROOKS DID NOT PUT ANY PRESSURE ON

12　YOU TO DO THIS. IS THAT RIGHT?

13　　A　I WOULDN'T CALL IT PRESSURE.　JUST ENTHUSIASM.　AT LEAST THIS

14　TIME.　IT WAS DIFFERENT THE SECOND TIME.

15　　Q　AND REVEREND ROOKS DID NOT TELL LIES TO GET YOU TO INVEST IN

16　THE B AND B BUSINESS?

17　　A　NOT AS SUCH.　LATER I LEARNED THAT THE BUSINESS WAS ALREADY

18　IN THE TANK WHEN HE FIRST STARTED TELLING ME ABOUT IT.　EVERYTHING

19　HE SAID TO ME PAINTED A PICTURE OF AN EXCITING FINANCIAL PROSPECT, A

20　START-UP BUSINESS WITH A VERY WORTHY GOAL.　HE NEVER SAID ANYTHING

21　ABOUT HOW THE BUSINESS REALLY STARTED OVER A YEAR AGO AND IT HAD

22　BEEN MISMANAGED AND WAS UNABLE TO PAY ITS BILLS AND WAS USING ITS

23　CAPITAL TO PAY DAILY OPERATING EXPENSES.　HE HELD THAT INFORMATION

24　BACK, WHICH AS FAR AS I AM CONCERNED WAS JUST AS BAD AS LYING TO ME.

25　　MS. RUMSDALE:

26　　MR. DU PRIEST, DO YOU HAVE THE SHARE CERTIFICATES THAT WERE

27　ISSUED TO MS. PETRILLO?

[Document page 17]

1　　MR. DUPRIEST:

2　　YES. COPIES WERE SUPPLIED TO YOU IN THE VERY FIRST PACKET OF

3　MATERIALS WE GAVE YOU IN OUR INITIAL DISCLOSURES.

4　　MS. RUMSDALE:

5　　AS I RECALL, THOSE CERTIFICATES WERE NOT SIGNED BY REVEREND

6　ROOKS. CAN YOU STIPULATE TO THAT SO THAT I DON'T NEED TO GO INTO

7　THAT HERE?

8　　MR. DUPRIEST:

9　　THEY WERE SIGNED BY HEATHER SEDALIA BURR AS A GENERAL PARTNER IN

10　THE LIMITED PARTNERSHIP OF R AND B LP.

11　　MS. RUMSDALE:

12　　AND BY NO ONE ELSE?

13　　MR. DUPRIEST:

14　　SO STIPULATED.

15　　BY MS. RUMSDALE:

16　　Q　NOW, MS. PETRILLO, WOULD YOU DESCRIBE THE CIRCUMSTANCES FOR

17　YOUR SUBSEQUENT INVESTMENT IN THIS BUSINESS?

18　　A　YES. WHEN I TOLD REVEREND ROOKS THAT I HAD PUT FOUR THOUSAND

19　DOLLARS INTO THE B AND B BUSINESS, HE DID NOT SEEM PARTICULARLY

20　INTERESTED.　OVER THE NEXT FEW WEEKS, HOWEVER, HE BEGAN CHIDING ME

21　FOR WHAT A TIMID PERSON I WAS AND HOW I REALLY NEEDED TO TAKE SOME

22　SIGNIFICANT RISKS AND EXPERIENCE THE FACT THAT I WOULD SURVIVE

23　BEFORE I COULD MAKE GENUINE INROADS INTO MY PROBLEMS. WHEN I WOULD

24　SPEAK WITH PRIDE ABOUT THE STEPS I HAD TAKEN, HE BELITTLED MY FOUR

25　THOUSAND DOLLAR INVESTMENT.　HE SAID I COULD CLEARLY AFFORD TO

26　INVEST MORE, WHICH WAS CORRECT. HE SAID I HAD MADE A TOKEN

27　INVESTMENT BUT IT WAS LIKE I WAS STILL WEARING MY DOWDY OLD CLOTHES.

1 HE ALSO BEGAN EXTOLLING THE HIGH-MINDEDNESS OF THIS INVESTMENT

2 BECAUSE OF ITS SPIRITUAL ASPECTS. AND THEN HE TOLD ME THAT I SHOULD

3 KNOW THAT THE R AND B LIMITED PARTNERSHIP WAS POISED ON THE BRINK OF

4 A STUNNING EXPANSION OF THE BUSINESS AND THAT THIS MIGHT BE MY LAST

5 CHANCE TO GET IN ON THE GROUND FLOOR OF A BUSINESS THAT COULD GIVE

6 ME FINANCIAL SECURITY FOR LIFE. HE SAID I REALLY NEEDED TO JUMP IN

7 WITH A SIGNIFICANT INVESTMENT, WHICH HE MADE CLEAR WOULD BE OVER ONE

8 HUNDRED THOUSAND DOLLARS. THESE LITTLE SPEECHES BEGAN TO DOMINATE

9 OUR SESSIONS IN NOVEMBER AND EARLY DECEMBER OF YR-02. I WAS RATHER

10 ANNOYED BY THIS DIVERSION OF OUR TIME TOGETHER TOWARDS THIS SINGLE

11 ISSUE. BUT YOU KNOW, DESPITE HOW MUCH HE ANNOYED AND SCARED ME, I

12 REALIZED THAT THESE WERE JUST TACTICS THAT HE USED IN ORDER TO HELP

13 ME HELP MYSELF. AND I HAD BECOME SO ATTACHED TO REVEREND ROOKS THAT

14 I THOUGHT HE COULD DO ANYTHING AND THAT I COULD DO NOTHING UNLESS I

15 FOLLOWED THE PATHS HE POINTED OUT. AND THAT'S HOW I CAME TO CALL

16 REVEREND BURR AND MAKE THE ADDITIONAL INVESTMENT OF $128,000. AND

17 OF COURSE IT WAS ONLY A COUPLE OF MONTHS LATER THAT I FOUND OUT THAT

18 R & B LP HAD FILED FOR BANKRUPTCY.

19   Q DID IT OCCUR TO YOU AT THE TIME THAT REVEREND ROOKS' BEHAVIOR

20 WAS SOMEWHAT UNUSUAL FOR A PASTORAL COUNSELOR?

21   A NOT AT THE TIME. I HAD NO BASIS FOR JUDGING HIS BEHAVIOR.

22   Q SO YOU DID NOT GO TO ANY OF THE OTHER PASTORS TO REPORT THESE

23 CONVERSATIONS WITH REVEREND ROOKS?

24   A NO.

25   Q AND YOU DID NOT GO TO REVEREND YUN THE SENIOR PASTOR AND TELL

26 HER THAT THERE WAS SOMETHING WRONG GOING ON IN REVEREND ROOKS'

27 COUNSELING PRACTICE, DID YOU?

[Document page 19]

1   A   NO, THAT CAME LATER.

2   Q   WHEN DID YOU FIRST TELL REVEREND YUN ABOUT REVEREND ROOKS'

3   CONDUCT CONNECTED WITH YOUR INVESTMENT WITH R AND B LP?

4   A   IN MAY OF LAST YEAR.

5   Q   WERE YOU STILL IN COUNSELING WITH REVEREND ROOKS AT THAT

6   TIME?

7   A   NO, IN APRIL I FOUND OUT ABOUT R & B'S BANKRUPTCY AND THEN

8   SOUGHT LEGAL COUNSEL. I BELIEVE I TERMINATED COUNSELING WITH

9   REVEREND ROOKS SHORTLY AFTER THAT, IN LATE APRIL.

10   Q   DID YOU EVER TALK WITH ANYONE ELSE WHO WAS A COUNSELING

11   CLIENT OF REVEREND ROOKS?

12   A   NOT THAT I KNOW OF. I MAY HAVE HAD CASUAL CONVERSATIONS WITH

13   ONE OR TWO OTHER CHURCH MEMBERS WHO HAPPENED TO HAVE BEEN IN

14   COUNSELING, BUT I DID NOT TALK TO ANYONE ABOUT COUNSELING AND

15   REVEREND ROOKS.

16   Q   PRIOR TO MAY OF YR-01, WHEN YOU COMPLAINED TO REVEREND YUN,

17   HAD YOU EVER HEARD ANYTHING FROM ANYONE ABOUT REVEREND ROOKS'

18   BEHAVIOR IN CONNECTION WITH PASTORAL COUNSELING?

19   A   NO.

20   Q   MS. PETRILLO, I KNOW THAT THE FINANCIAL LOSS YOU SUFFERED AS

21   A RESULT OF THIS INVESTMENT IS EXTREMELY UPSETTING TO YOU, AND I AM

22   SURE THAT IT RATHER BADLY COLORS YOUR MEMORY OF YOUR EXPERIENCE WITH

23   REVEREND ROOKS. BUT IT DOES SEEM TO ME THAT SOME OF THE OUTCOMES

24   THAT YOU EXPERIENCED AS A RESULT OF YOUR THERAPY WITH REVEREND ROOKS

25   WERE BENEFICIAL. WOULD YOU AGREE?

26   A   SURE. APART FROM ALL THIS WEIRDNESS ABOUT INVESTMENT AND THE

27   FACT THAT I LOST A LOT OF MONEY, I WOULD SAY THAT I CHANGED A LOT

1 AND GAINED A LOT AS A RESULT OF MY THERAPY WITH REVEREND ROOKS.

2 THOUGH IT ALL SEEMS OVER-SHADOWED NOW BY THE WAY HE BETRAYED ME.

3 AND IT DOESN'T GET ME BACK THE MONEY I LOST. THAT'S WHAT THIS

4 LAWSUIT IS ABOUT.

5   Q MS. PETRILLO, APART FROM THE TOPICS THAT CAME UP IN YOUR

6 PASTORAL COUNSELING, I WOULD LIKE YOU TO DESCRIBE REVEREND ROOKS'

7 METHODOLOGY AS A COUNSELOR. YOU MENTIONED THAT AT FIRST HE WAS

8 SUPPORTIVE AND LATER HE BECAME WHAT YOU CALLED CONFRONTATIONAL. YOU

9 MENTIONED THAT HE SOMETIMES GAVE YOU BIBLE PASSAGES TO TAKE HOME.

10 WHAT OTHER METHODS DID HE USE?

11   A   SOMETIMES HE WOULD HAVE ME DO GUIDED MEDITATIONS. SOMETIMES

12 WE WOULD PRAY TOGETHER. HE WAS CONSTANTLY ASKING ME HOW THINGS MADE

13 ME FEEL. I GUESS I JUST FOCUSED ON WHAT HAPPENED AND HE WANTED ME TO

14 BE AWARE OF MY FEELINGS.

15   Q WERE THERE ANY BASIC THEMES OF THE GUIDED MEDITATIONS?

16   A WELL, HE WOULD TAKE ME TO A VERY PEACEFUL PLACE. MAYBE THE

17 WOODS OR A LAKE OR SOMEWHERE REALLY PEACEFUL. AND THEN SOMETHING

18 WOULD HAPPEN. MAYBE A WILD ANIMAL WOULD APPEAR. AND HE WOULD SUGGEST

19 THAT I ARM MYSELF AGAINST ALL DANGER AND I WOULD BE PROTECTED. OR I

20 WOULD BE SURROUNDED BY AN INVISIBLE SHIELD OF LOVE AND NOTHING COULD

21 HARM ME. AFTER A WHILE HE WOULD GUIDE ME BACK AND HELP ME NOTICE HOW

22 STRONG AND SELF-CONFIDENT I FELT.

23   Q WERE THERE ANY BASIC THEMES OF THE BIBLE PASSAGES HE WOULD

24 BRING UP?

25   A   IT WAS MOSTLY NEW TESTAMENT STUFF ABOUT MANKIND'S NEW

26 BEGINNING WITH CHRIST AND HOW GOD WOULD CONFER HIS BLESSINGS IN THE

27 MOST PARADOXICAL WAYS. HE WAS BIG ON THE SERMON ON THE MOUNT.

[Document page 21]

1   SOMETIMES HE WOULD READ FROM THE PSALMS. THE ONE I REMEMBER THAT HE

2   BROUGHT UP THE MOST WAS THE ONE THAT BEGINS MAKE A JOYFUL NOISE UNTO

3   THE LORD AND SERVE THE LORD WITH GLADNESS. HE TOLD ME THAT GOD WOULD

4   BE MUCH MORE PLEASED WITH ME IF I MADE MORE NOISE, AS HE PUT IT. IT

5   WAS JUST A FIGURE OF SPEECH BUT IT MEANT A LOT TO ME. HE WANTED ME

6   TO BE WHAT HE CALLED A NOISY EMPLOYEE AND A NOISY DRESSER AND A

7   NOISY INVESTOR. HE WANTED ME TO APPROACH MY LIFE WITH GLADNESS AND

8   LOOK AT MY MORE DARING AND SELF-CONFIDENT LIFE STYLE AS A FORM OF

9   WORSHIP THAT WOULD BE PLEASING TO GOD.

10   Q   DID REVEREND ROOKS EVER REFER TO OTHER PASSAGES FROM

11   LITERATURE OR RELIGIOUS TEXTS?

12   A   NOT TOO MUCH. OCCASIONALLY HE WOULD READ POETRY. HE LIKED

13   KHALIL GIBRAN, AND I DON'T THINK HE WAS A CHRISTIAN BUT HE WAS A

14   VERY BEAUTIFUL AND INSIGHTFUL WRITER.

15   Q   DO YOU THINK YOUR PASTORAL COUNSELING WOULD HAVE BEEN AS

16   EFFECTIVE IF IT HAD JUST SKIPPED THE RELIGIOUS THEMES?

17   A   NO. THOSE THEMES WERE IMPORTANT TO ME.

18   Q   DO YOU THINK YOUR PASTORAL COUNSELING WOULD HAVE BEEN AS

19   EFFECTIVE IF IT HAD USED HINDU THEMES AS OPPOSED TO CHRISTIAN

20   THEMES, OR ISLAMIC THEMES OR SOME OTHER RELIGION OUTSIDE

21   CHRISTIANITY?

22   A   WELL, I HARDLY KNOW. I AM A CHRISTIAN AND SO CHRISTIAN THEMES

23   MEAN THE MOST TO ME. I DON'T KNOW ENOUGH ABOUT OTHER RELIGIONS TO

24   KNOW WHAT THEY HAVE THAT MIGHT HAVE BEEN HELPFUL TO ME.

25   MS. RUMSDALE:

26   I HAVE NO FURTHER QUESTIONS AT THIS TIME. THANK YOU MS.

27   PETRILLO. MR. DUPRIEST DID YOU WANT TO CROSS-EXAMINE?

[handwritten margin note: Theme of counseling]

1   MR. DUPRIEST:

2   YES, BUT COULD WE HAVE A SHORT RECESS FIRST?

3   MS. RUMSDALE:

4   CERTAINLY.

5   [DEPOSITION IN RECESS FROM 3:05 P.M. UNTIL 3:18 P.M.]

6   EXAMINATION ON BEHALF OF THE PLAINTIFF

7   BY MR. DUPRIEST:

8   Q   MS. PETRILLO, I AM HAVING A HARD TIME SEEING HOW YOUR STYLE

9   OF DRESS AND WEARING MAKEUP AND INVESTING IN EQUITIES VERSUS CD'S

10   HAS ANYTHING TO DO WITH YOUR RELIGIOUS BELIEFS. ISN'T IT QUITE

11   POSSIBLE THAT MR. ROOKS' TECHNIQUES WOULD HAVE HAD EXACTLY THE SAME

12   EFFECT WITHOUT THE RELIGIOUS TRAPPINGS?

13   A   MAYBE SO. I DON'T KNOW.

14   Q   ARE YOU FAMILIAR WITH ANY OF THE SECULAR WRITINGS ABOUT

15   COUNSELING AND PSYCHOTHERAPY?

16   A   NO.

17   Q   ARE YOU AWARE THAT ALL OF THE TECHNIQUES THAT REVEREND ROOKS

18   USED CAN BE FOUND IN ONE OR MORE BOOKS ABOUT COUNSELING, AND NOT

19   PASTORAL COUNSELING BUT JUST REGULAR SECULAR COUNSELING?

20   A   NO.

21   Q   DID REVEREND ROOKS EVER EXPLAIN TO YOU THAT HIS

22   RECOMMENDATION THAT YOU INVEST IN HIS BUSINESS PLACED HIM IN A

23   POSITION OF A CONFLICT OF INTEREST AND SUGGEST THAT YOU MIGHT WANT

24   TO SEE AN INDEPENDENT COUNSELOR BEFORE YOU DECIDED WHETHER OR NOT TO

25   INVEST IN HIS BUSINESS?

26   A   NO.

27   Q   DID REVEREND ROOKS EVER MENTION HIS CONTACTS WITH OTHER

[Document page 23]

1   MEMBERS OF THE PASTORAL STAFF AT YOUR CHURCH?

2   A   ONLY IN A VERY CASUAL WAY. NOTHING IN PARTICULAR.

3   Q   HOW CLOSE WAS HE WITH REVEREND YUN?

4   A   I THINK HE WAS PRETTY CLOSE, BUT I DON'T KNOW FOR SURE. I

5   KNOW HE OFTEN SPOKE OF CONVERSATIONS WITH HER. HE ACTED AS IF HE

6   LIKED AND RESPECTED REVEREND YUN.

7   Q   DID HE EVER TALK ABOUT CONVERSATIONS WITH REVEREND YUN IN

8   WHICH THEY DISCUSSED HIS PASTORAL COUNSELING WORK?

9   A   WELL I KNOW THAT REVEREND YUN WAS CONCERNED THAT REVEREND

10 ROOKS WAS PUTTING IN TOO MANY HOURS AND THAT HE SHOULD CUT BACK. IT

11 SEEMED LIKE HE WAS ALWAYS AVAILABLE WHENEVER ANYONE NEEDED HIM, DAY

12 OR NIGHT. I THINK REVEREND YUN WAS AFRAID REVEREND ROOKS MIGHT BURN

13 HIMSELF OUT.

14   Q   DID REVEREND ROOKS SAY THAT?

15   A   YES.

16   Q   DID HE EVER TALK ABOUT SHARING WITH REVEREND YUN ANY

17 INFORMATION ABOUT HIS COUNSELING CLIENTS AND THEIR PARTICULAR

18 PROBLEMS?

19   A   NO. IT WOULD SURPRISE ME IF HE DID. HE TOLD ME THAT OUR

20 SESSIONS WERE CONFIDENTIAL, AND I WOULD NOT EXPECT HIM TO DISCUSS

21 HIS CLIENTS WITH ANYONE ELSE. I NEVER HEARD OF HIM SAYING ANYTHING

22 LIKE THAT.

23   Q   SO FAR AS YOU KNOW, DID REVEREND YUN EVER INQUIRE OF REVEREND

24 ROOKS ABOUT HOW HIS COUNSELING PRACTICE WAS GOING?

25   A   I REALLY WOULDN'T KNOW OTHER THAN HER CONCERN ABOUT HIS

26 WORKING TOO HARD.

27   Q   DID YOU HAVE THE IMPRESSION THAT REVEREND ROOKS WAS BEING

1   SUPERVISED BY ANYONE ELSE?

2   A   NOT REALLY.

3   Q   WHAT IS THE TOTAL AMOUNT THAT YOU INVESTED IN R & B, LP?

4   A $132,000.

5   Q   HOW MUCH OF THAT DID YOU LOSE?

6   A   ALL OF IT. WELL, PROBABLY. I DON'T THINK THE BANKRUPTCY IS

7   ALL FINISHED, BUT THE BANKRUPTCY TRUSTEE SAID I COULD NOT EXPECT TO

8   RECEIVE ANYTHING. I FILED A CLAIM, BUT I DON'T THINK I'LL GET

9   ANYTHING BACK.

10   MR. DUPRIEST:

11   THANK YOU, MS. PETRILLO.

12   MS. RUMSDALE:

13   MR. AHERN, WOULD YOU PLEASE NOTE THAT MR. DUPRIEST AND I HAVE

14 ENTERED THE USUAL STIPULATIONS AS TO THE TRANSCRIPTION, SIGNING, AND

15 FILING OF THIS DEPOSITION?

16   MR. DUPRIEST:

17   THAT'S CORRECT.

18   MS. RUMSDALE:

19   THAT CONCLUDES THIS DEPOSITION.

20   (AT 3:38 P.M., APRIL 7, YR-00, THE DEPOSITION OF ERNESTINE

21 PETRILLO WAS ADJOURNED.)

22 //

23 //

24 //

25 //

26 //

27 //

[Document page 25]

1   REPORTER'S CERTIFICATE

2   I, LEONARD AHERN, OFFICIAL COURT REPORTER OF THE STATE OF

3   ALABAMA, HEREBY CERTIFY THAT THE FOREGOING DEPOSITION OF ERNESTINE

4   PETRILLO WAS TAKEN BEFORE ME AT THE TIME AND PLACE HEREIN SET FORTH,

5   AT WHICH TIME THE WITNESS WAS PUT ON OATH BY ME;

6   THAT THE TESTIMONY OF THE WITNESS AND ALL OBJECTIONS MADE AT THE

7   TIME OF EXAMINATION WERE RECORDED STENOGRAPHICALLY BY ME, AND WERE

8   THEREAFTER TRANSCRIBED UNDER MY DIRECT SUPERVISION.

9   I FURTHER CERTIFY THAT I AM NEITHER COUNSEL FOR NOR RELATED TO

10   ANY PARTY TO SAID ACTION, NOR AM I IN ANYWISE INTERESTED IN THE

11   OUTCOME THEREOF.

12   IN WITNESS WHEREOF, I HAVE SUBSCRIBED MY NAME ON APRIL 13, YR-

13   00.

Leonard Ahern

Emily Rumsdale
Miller, Eldridge & Pasternak
13304 Bald Mountain Parkway
Bald Mountain, Alabama 36918
Telephone (934) 485-9000

UNITED STATES DISTRICT COURT
FILED
May 14, YR-00
WESTERN DISTRICT OF ALABAMA

Attorney for Defendants
Rev. Harriett Yun and
Bald Mountain Community Church

In the
United States District Court
for the Western District of Alabama

Ernestine Petrillo,	)	
	)	
Plaintiff	)	
v.	)	Civil Action No. 00-85FD
	)	
Linwood Rooks, et al.	)	
	)	
Defendants	)	

ANSWER OF DEFENDANTS BALD MOUNTAIN COMMUNITY CHURCH AND REV. HARRIETT YUN

This answer is filed on behalf of the defendants Bald Mountain Community Church (hereinafter referred to as "BMCC") and Rev. Harriett Yun. These defendants are hereinafter referred to collectively as "Defendants."

1.   Defendants are without knowledge or information sufficient to form a belief as to the truth of paragraph 1 of the complaint.

[Document page 1]

2.   Defendants admit the second, third, and fourth sentences of paragraph 2 of the complaint. They deny the first and fifth sentences of paragraph 2 of the complaint.

3.   Paragraph 3 of the complaint does not call for an answer.

4.   Defendants deny the last sentence of paragraph 4 of the complaint; deny that the remaining sentences of paragraph 4 are a complete description of Rev. Yun's responsibilities as Senior Pastor of Bald Mountain Community Church; and otherwise admit paragraph 4.

5.   Defendants are without knowledge or information sufficient to form a belief as to the truth of paragraph 5 of the complaint.

6.   Defendants admit paragraph 6 of the complaint.

7-24.   Defendants are without knowledge or information sufficient to form a belief as to the truth of paragraphs 7 through 24 of the complaint.

25.   Defendants admit the first sentence of paragraph 25 and deny the remainder of paragraph 25 of the complaint.

26.   Defendants deny paragraph 26 of the complaint.

27-33.   Defendants deny paragraphs 27 through 33 of the complaint.

FIRST DEFENSE

34.   Because plaintiff and all defendants are citizens of Alabama, this court lacks subject matter jurisdiction of this action pursuant to 28 U.S.C. § 1332.

[Document page 2]

SECOND DEFENSE

35. Counts Four, Five, and Six of the complaint fail to state claims upon which relief can be granted.

THIRD DEFENSE

36. A judgment granting the plaintiff any form of relief against Defendants on the basis of the claims set forth in Counts Five and Six of the complaint, as well as the very process of adjudicating Counts Five and Six of the complaint, would violate the First Amendment of the United States Constitution.

FOURTH DEFENSE

37. A judgment granting the plaintiff any form of relief against Defendants on the basis of the claims set forth in Counts Five and Six of the complaint, as well as the very process of adjudicating Counts Five and Six of the complaint, would violate Amendment No. 622 of the Alabama Constitution ("Alabama Religious Freedom Amendment").

FIFTH DEFENSE

38.   The plaintiff failed to invoke and exhaust ecclesiastical remedies available to her within BMCC, and, therefore, her claims are not ripe for adjudication, her claims are not justiciable, and this court lacks subject matter jurisdiction pursuant to Article III of the United States Constitution.

[Document page 3]

Dated: May 13, YR-00

Respectfully submitted,

Emily Rumsdale
_____

Emily Rumsdale

Miller, Eldridge & Pasternak
13304 Bald Mountain Parkway
Bald Mountain, Alabama 36918
Telephone (934) 485-9000

Attorney for Defendants
Rev. Harriett Yun and
Bald Mountain Community Church

CERTIFICATE OF SERVICE

I certify that on this 13th day of May, YR-00, I served the foregoing Answer of

Defendants Bald Mountain Community Church and Rev. Harriett Yun upon the

plaintiff by causing a copy thereof to be mailed, first class postage prepaid, to

the attorney for the plaintiff, Armand DuPriest, at Wilson & DuPriest, 900 Maple

Lane, Bald Mountain, Alabama 36918.

Emily Rumsdale

Emily Rumsdale

Miller, Eldridge & Pasternak
13304 Bald Mountain Parkway
Bald Mountain, Alabama 36918
Telephone (934) 485-9000

Attorney for Defendants
Rev. Harriett Yun and
Bald Mountain Community Church

IN THE UNITED STATES DISTRICT COURT
FOR THE WESTERN DISTRICT OF ALABAMA

```
┌─────────────────────────────────────┐
│      UNITED STATES DISTRICT COURT    │
│             FILED                    │
│         June 3, YR-00                │
│     WESTERN DISTRICT OF ALABAMA      │
└─────────────────────────────────────┘
```

ERNESTINE PETRILLO

    PLAINTIFF

VS.   CIVIL ACTION NO. 00-85FD

LINWOOD ROOKS, ET AL.

    DEFENDANTS

DEPOSITION OF LINWOOD ROOKS

TAKEN BY PLAINTIFF AT 900 MAPLE LANE, BALD MOUNTAIN, ALABAMA,
COMMENCING AT 10:00 A.M., MAY 20, YR-00, BEFORE LEONARD AHERN,
CERTIFIED STENOGRAPHIC REPORTER.

APPEARANCES:

FOR PLAINTIFF:

WILSON & DUPRIEST

    BY: ARMAND DUPRIEST, ESQ.

900 MAPLE LANE
BALD MOUNTAIN, ALABAMA 36918
TELEPHONE (934) 333-2541

FOR DEFENDANTS HARRIETT YUN AND BALD MOUNTAIN COMMUNITY CHURCH:

MILLER, ELDRIDGE & PASTERNAK

    BY: EMILY RUMSDALE, ESQ.

13304 BALD MOUNTAIN PARKWAY
BALD MOUNTAIN, ALABAMA 36918
TELEPHONE (934) 485-9000

FOR THE WITNESS, LINWOOD ROOKS:

BASCOM JESSUP-FRANKLIN, ESQ.

12520 BALD MOUNTAIN PARKWAY
BALD MOUNTAIN, ALABAMA 36918
TELEPHONE (934) 485-2620

[Document page 1]

1   BALD MOUNTAIN, ALABAMA, MAY 20, YR-00

2   LINWOOD ROOKS

3   HAVING BEEN DULY SWORN, TESTIFIED AS FOLLOWS:

4   EXAMINATION ON BEHALF OF THE PLAINTIFF

5   MR. DUPRIEST:

6   GOOD MORNING. MY NAME IS ARMAND DUPRIEST. I REPRESENT THE

7 PLAINTIFF ERNESTINE PETRILLO IN THE CASE OF PETRILLO VERSUS ROOKS AND

8 OTHERS, CIVIL ACTION NO. 00-85 IN THE UNITED STATES DISTRICT COURT FOR

9 THE WESTERN DISTRICT OF ALABAMA. THIS MORNING PLAINTIFF WILL TAKE THE

10 DEPOSITION OF REVEREND LINWOOD ROOKS, WHO IS NAMED AS A DEFENDANT IN

11 THIS ACTION BUT WHO HAS PREVIOUSLY INDICATED THAT HE DOES NOT INTEND

12 TO CONTEST THIS ACTION. WE SERVED A SUBPOENA ON MR. ROOKS COMMANDING

13 HIS PRESENCE AT THIS DEPOSITION, AND MR. ROOKS IS PRESENT. MR. ROOKS

14 IS ACCOMPANIED BY COUNSEL. BASS, WOULD YOU LIKE TO INTRODUCE YOURSELF

15 FOR THE RECORD?

16   MR. JESSUP-FRANKLIN:

17   I AM BASCOM JESSUP-FRANKLIN, A MEMBER OF THE BAR OF ALABAMA, WITH

18 LAW OFFICES AT 12520 BALD MOUNTAIN PARKWAY HERE IN BALD MOUNTAIN. I

19 REPRESENT MR. LINWOOD ROOKS, THE DEPONENT. WHILE I HAVE THE FLOOR, MR.

20 DUPRIEST, I WOULD LIKE TO MAKE A STATEMENT ON BEHALF OF MR. ROOKS, DO

21 YOU MIND?

22   MR. DUPRIEST:

23   NOT AT ALL. GO RIGHT AHEAD.

24   MR. JESSUP-FRANKLIN:

25   AS YOU KNOW, MR. ROOKS HAS BEEN CRIMINALLY CHARGED WITH VIOLATING

26 THE ALABAMA SECURITIES LAW IN CONNECTION WITH THE SAME TRANSACTIONS

27 THAT ARE THE SUBJECT OF THIS LAW SUIT. THEREFORE, MR. ROOKS WILL

[Document page 2]

1 EXERCISE HIS FIFTH AMENDMENT RIGHT NOT TO TESTIFY ABOUT ANYTHING

2 HAVING TO DO WITH THOSE TRANSACTIONS OR THAT MAY IN ANY OTHER WAY TEND

3 TO INCRIMINATE HIM. FURTHERMORE, INSOFAR AS MR. ROOKS' COMMUNICATIONS

4 WITH MS. PETRILLO WERE IN HIS PROFESSIONAL CAPACITY AS A CLERGYMAN,

5 MR. ROOKS WILL STAND ON HIS PRIVILEGE NOT TO REVEAL THOSE

6 COMMUNICATIONS AS PROVIDED IN ALABAMA RULES OF EVIDENCE RULE 505. HE

7 IS CERTAINLY WILLING TO TESTIFY TO GENERAL BACKGROUND INFORMATION IF

8 THAT WOULD BE HELPFUL.

9   MR. DUPRIEST:

10   YOUR POSITION IS CLEAR. AS YOU MAY KNOW WE TAKE THE POSITION THAT

11 THE RULE 505 PRIVILEGE DOES NOT APPLY IN THIS KIND OF SITUATION. WE

12 HAVE A MOTION BEFORE DISTRICT JUDGE DRAFTER ON THAT VERY QUESTION. FOR

13 NOW, WE WILL CONDITIONALLY HONOR YOUR ASSERTION OF THE PRIVILEGE BUT

14 WITHOUT PREJUDICE TO OUR CALLING MR. ROOKS BACK IN THE EVENT JUDGE

15 DRAFTER RULES AGAINST THE APPLICATION OF THE MINISTERIAL PRIVILEGE IN

16 THESE CIRCUMSTANCES. NEITHER THE RULE 505 PRIVILEGE NOR THE FIFTH

17 AMENDMENT PRIVILEGE PREVENTS MR. ROOKS FROM BEING CALLED AS A WITNESS

18 AND WE INTEND TO PROCEED WITH THIS DEPOSITION, SUBJECT TO MR. ROOKS'

19 ASSERTION OF EITHER PRIVILEGE IN RESPONSE TO SPECIFIC QUESTIONS. IS

20 THAT AGREEABLE?

21   MR. JESSUP-FRANKLIN:

22   WELL, LET'S SEE HOW IT GOES. IT'S AGREEABLE TO GET STARTED ON THAT

23 BASIS.

24   MR. DUPRIEST:

25   I ALSO WANTED TO INDICATE THAT THE OTHER PERSONS PRESENT AT THIS

26 DEPOSITION BESIDES MR. ROOKS, MR. JESSUP-FRANKLIN, AND MYSELF, ARE

27 EMILY RUMSDALE, COUNSEL FOR THE DEFENDANTS BALD MOUNTAIN COMMUNITY

[Document page 3]

1 CHURCH AND THE REVEREND HARRIETT YUN, AND ALSO THE COURT REPORTER MR.

2 AHERN.

3   BY MR. DUPRIEST:

4   Q WOULD YOU PLEASE STATE YOUR FULL NAME FOR THE RECORD AND SPELL

5   YOUR LAST NAME?

6   A MY NAME IS LINWOOD ROOKS. ROOKS IS SPELLED R-O-O-K-S.

7 THE REPORTER:

8 IS YOUR FIRST NAME SPELLED L-I-N-W-O-O-D?

9 THE WITNESS:

10 YES.

11 BY MR. DUPRIEST:

12   Q AM I CORRECT IN SAYING THAT YOU ARE NAMED AS A DEFENDANT IN THIS

13 ACTION BUT HAVE ELECTED NOT TO DEFEND AND NOT TO PARTICIPATE IN ANY

14 WAY EXCEPT AS MAY BE REQUIRED BY COURT ORDER?

15   A THAT'S CORRECT.

16   [PRELIMINARY QUESTIONS. SEE FOOTNOTE 4, PAGE 60, SUPRA.]

17   * * *

18   Q MR. ROOKS, WOULD YOU PLEASE TELL US SOMETHING ABOUT YOUR

19 PERSONAL AND EDUCATIONAL BACKGROUND?

20   A I WAS BORN AND RAISED IN SEDONA, ARIZONA. MY DAD WAS A

21 PHOTOGRAPHER AND MOM A SCULPTOR. I HAVE TWO SISTERS AND A BROTHER. I

22 AM NOW 42 YEARS OLD. MY UNDERGRADUATE EDUCATION WAS AT KENYON COLLEGE

23 IN GAMBIER, OHIO. AFTER RECEIVING MY UNDERGRADUATE DEGREE IN YR-20, I

24 WORKED IN VARIOUS JOBS, MOSTLY IN THE COMMUNICATIONS INDUSTRY, TRYING

25 TO FIGURE OUT WHAT CAREER TO PURSUE. INCREASINGLY, I FELT DRAWN TO

26 THE MINISTRY, AND SO I ENROLLED IN TRINITY THEOLOGICAL SEMINARY IN

27 EVANSVILLE, INDIANA. I GRADUATED FROM SEMINARY IN YR-12 AND WAS

[Document page 4]

1 ORDAINED AS A PRIEST OF THE EPISCOPAL CHURCH IN YR-11. I WORKED IN

2 PARISH MINISTRY IN TWO DIFFERENT EPISCOPAL PARISHES OVER THE NEXT

3 THREE YEARS. INCREASINGLY I CAME TO REALIZE THAT MY TRUE CALLING WAS

4 TO PASTORAL COUNSELING. I DID SOME COUNSELING WORK AS A PARISH PRIEST,

5 BUT I REALIZED THAT I NEEDED MORE TRAINING. SO IN AUGUST YR-08 I

6 ENTERED A DOCTORAL PROGRAM IN PASTORAL COUNSELING WHICH I COMPLETED

7 TWO YEARS LATER WITH A DOCTOR OF THEOLOGY DEGREE. TO BE FULLY

8 QUALIFIED, I NEEDED SUPERVISED CLINICAL EXPERIENCE, AND SO I APPLIED

9 TO AND WAS ACCEPTED AS AN ASSOCIATE COUNSELOR AT A COUNSELING PRACTICE

10 IN CINCINNATI, OHIO. I WORKED THERE AND COMPLETED MY SUPERVISED HOURS

11 IN YR-04. I CONTINUED WORKING IN THAT PRACTICE AS A PASTORAL COUNSELOR

12 UNTIL JUNE OF YR-03, WHEN I WAS CALLED TO BE ASSOCIATE PASTOR AND HEAD

13 OF THE PASTORAL COUNSELING CENTER AT BALD MOUNTAIN COMMUNITY CHURCH. I

14 WORKED THERE UNTIL JULY 1, YR-01, WHEN I RESIGNED TO PURSUE OTHER

15 INTERESTS.

16   Q   WHO SETS THE REQUIREMENTS FOR BEING A PASTORAL COUNSELOR AND

17 WHAT ARE THOSE REQUIREMENTS?

18   A   I'M AFRAID YOUR SIMPLE QUESTION CALLS FOR A COMPLICATED ANSWER.

19 I'LL TRY TO BE BRIEF. THERE IS NO STATE LICENSURE FOR PASTORAL

20 COUNSELORS. SOME INDIVIDUALS WHO PRACTICE PASTORAL COUNSELING CHOOSE

21 TO BECOME LICENSED AS CLINICAL PSYCHOLOGISTS, MARRIAGE AND FAMILY

22 THERAPISTS, AND OTHER DESIGNATIONS, BUT THAT IS NOT REQUIRED UNDER THE

23 LAWS OF ANY STATE TO PRACTICE AS A PASTORAL COUNSELOR. A FEW

24 DENOMINATIONS HAVE DETAILED STANDARDS FOR PASTORAL COUNSELORS. OTHERS

25 HAVE NO STANDARDS WHATSOEVER. FINALLY, THERE ARE THE PROFESSIONAL

26 ASSOCIATIONS. THERE IS ONE MAJOR NATIONAL ORGANIZATION OF PASTORAL

27 COUNSELORS AND OVER A HALF-DOZEN SMALLER ORGANIZATIONS OF PASTORAL

[Document page 5]

1   COUNSELORS. MOST OF THESE ORGANIZATIONS HAVE CRITERIA FOR MEMBERSHIP,

2   MAINTAIN CODES OF GOOD PRACTICE, AND THE LIKE. AS FOR ME, I AM A

3   MEMBER OF THE NORTH AMERICAN COLLEGE OF PASTORAL COUNSELORS. I

4   SATISFIED ALL THE REQUIREMENTS FOR MEMBERSHIP AND WAS ADMITTED TO

5   MEMBERSHIP IN YR-02.

6   Q   IF A PASTORAL COUNSELOR IS SUSPECTED OF PROFESSIONAL MISCONDUCT,

7   TO WHOM SHOULD AN AGGRIEVED CLIENT TURN?

8   A   FIRST TO THE CHURCH WITH WHICH THE PASTORAL COUNSELOR IS

9   AFFILIATED. TO THE RELEVANT PROFESSIONAL ORGANIZATION, IF ANY. AND IF

10   THE COUNSELOR IS PROFESSIONALLY LICENSED IN AN ALLIED FIELD, TO THE

11   LICENSING AUTHORITIES.

12   Q   ARE THERE GENERALLY ACCEPTED CODES OF PROFESSIONAL CONDUCT FOR

13   PASTORAL COUNSELORS?

14   A   THERE ARE SEVERAL. MOST OF THEM ARE MANDATORY ON MEMBERS OF THE

15   ORGANIZATION BY WHICH THE CODE WAS ISSUED AND SOME ARE USED AS GUIDES

16   OUTSIDE THE ORGANIZATION. WHILE THERE ARE SEVERAL DIFFERENT CODES,

17   MOST OF THEM AGREE ON THE ESSENTIALS, SUCH AS CONFIDENTIALITY,

18   LOYALTY, AVOIDANCE OF SEXUAL AND ROMANTIC RELATIONSHIPS, AND THE LIKE.

19   Q   DO ANY OF THE CODES SAY ANYTHING ABOUT BUSINESS DEALINGS WITH

20   CLIENTS?

21   A   NOT TO MY KNOWLEDGE. AT LEAST NOT SPECIFICALLY.

22   Q   WHAT DO YOU CONSIDER TO BE THE ETHICAL CONSTRAINTS ON BUSINESS

23   DEALINGS WITH CLIENTS?

24   A   AS LONG AS THERE IS FULL DISCLOSURE AND THE COUNSELOR IS ACTING

25   FOR THE BEST INTERESTS OF THE CLIENT THERE SHOULD BE NO PROBLEM.

26   Q   HOW DID YOU FIRST HEAR ABOUT BALD MOUNTAIN COMMUNITY CHURCH?

27   A   IN FEBRUARY OR MARCH OF YR-03, MY BOSS AND MENTOR, DR. LELAND

1 LAMPREY NORTH, TOLD ME THAT HE HAD RECEIVED AN INQUIRY FROM A

2 COMMUNITY CHURCH IN ALABAMA THAT WAS LOOKING FOR A FULL TIME PASTORAL

3 COUNSELOR. THE MINISTER WAS AN OLD FRIEND OF HIS AND HE ENCOURAGED ME

4 TO APPLY FOR THE POSITION. I HAD A FEW TELEPHONE CONVERSATIONS WITH

5 REVEREND YUN, THE SENIOR PASTOR, AND THEN I RECEIVED A LETTER FROM THE

6 CHAIR WOMAN OF THE CHURCH COUNCIL INVITING ME FOR AN INTERVIEW. I WENT

7 DOWN TO BALD MOUNTAIN AND PARTICIPATED IN A DAY AND A HALF'S WORTH OF

8 INTERVIEWS. I LIKED THE PEOPLE, I REALLY LIKED THE COMMUNITY, AND I

9 WAS VERY FAVORABLY IMPRESSED BY THE CHURCH'S PROGRAMS. AND SO I WAS

10 DELIGHTED WHEN I RECEIVED A FORMAL CALL TO BE AN ASSOCIATE PASTOR OF

11 THAT CHURCH AND HEAD OF THE PASTORAL COUNSELING CENTER.

12   Q   DO YOU KNOW THE DATES?

13   A   THE CALL LETTER WAS ISSUED MAY 29 AND I SENT BACK MY LETTER OF

14 ACCEPTANCE ON JUNE 14 OR 15. I ACTUALLY STARTED WORKING THERE ON THE

15 FIRST OF JULY YR-03.

16   Q   IF YOU ARE ORDAINED AS AN EPISCOPAL PRIEST, ISN'T IT SOMEWHAT

17 IRREGULAR FOR YOU TO BE SERVING AS A PASTOR IN A NON-EPISCOPAL CHURCH?

18   A   NOT AT ALL. MY HOLY ORDERS ARE FULLY INTACT. HOWEVER, I FOLLOWED

19 THE PROCEDURE TO BE RELEASED FROM THE AUTHORITY OF MY BISHOP SO AS TO

20 BE ABLE TO AFFILIATE MYSELF WITH ANOTHER CHURCH. BALD MOUNTAIN

21 COMMUNITY CHURCH IS ABOUT AS NON-DENOMINATIONAL A CHURCH AS I HAVE

22 EVER SEEN. WE HAVE SEVERAL ASSOCIATE AND ASSISTANT PASTORS, AND I

23 DON'T THINK ANY TWO CAME UP IN THE MINISTRY IN THE SAME DENOMINATION.

24 PASTOR YUN WAS ORDAINED BY THE DISCIPLES OF CHRIST. PASTOR MARTIN WAS

25 A METHODIST MINISTER. PASTOR ALLGOOD A LUTHERAN. PASTOR WARD GREW UP

26 AND WAS ORDAINED IN THE SOUTHERN BAPTIST CHURCH.

27   Q   IS THERE ANY COMMON DOGMA OR PROFESSION OF FAITH THAT BINDS YOU

1 ALL TOGETHER?

2   A WE ALL SUBMIT OURSELVES TO THE AUTHORITY OF HOLY SCRIPTURE,

3 WHICH WE ALL PROFESS AS THE DIVINE WORD OF GOD. WE STRONGLY BELIEVE,

4 HOWEVER, THAT THE CHURCH HAS NO BUSINESS TELLING PEOPLE WHAT TO

5 BELIEVE OR HOW TO INTERPRET THE SCRIPTURES. EACH PASTOR OF BALD

6 MOUNTAIN COMMUNITY CHURCH AND EACH MEMBER IS FULLY QUALIFIED TO

7 INTERPRET THE BIBLE BY HIS OR HER OWN LIGHTS AND TO SUBSCRIBE TO ANY

8 SET OF BELIEFS THEY WANT TO.

9   Q APART FROM YOUR INITIAL CONVERSATIONS WITH PASTOR YUN AND THE

10 DAY AND A HALF OF INTERVIEWS, DO YOU KNOW WHAT OTHER PROCESSES THE

11 BALD MOUNTAIN CHURCH FOLLOWED TO DETERMINE YOUR QUALIFICATIONS AND

12 COMPETENCY TO SERVE AS THE HEAD OF THE CHURCH'S PASTORAL COUNSELING

13 CENTER?

14   A I KNOW THAT PASTOR YUN TALKED WITH MY MENTOR, DR. NORTH. OTHER

15 THAN THAT, I DON'T KNOW.

16   Q DO YOU KNOW WHETHER PASTOR YUN OR ANYONE ELSE AT BALD MOUNTAIN

17 CHURCH WAS MADE AWARE OF THE SIDE BUSINESS THAT YOU STARTED UP WHILE

18 YOU WERE WORKING IN DR. NORTH'S COUNSELING PRACTICE?

19   MR. JESSUP-FRANKLIN:

20   JUST A MINUTE, PLEASE. YOUR QUESTION ASSUMES A FACT NOT IN

21 EVIDENCE. MY CLIENT AND I NEED TO KNOW WHAT BUSINESS YOU ARE REFERRING

22 TO BEFORE RESPONDING TO THAT QUESTION.

23   MR. DUPRIEST:

24   MY QUESTION RELATES TO THE BED AND BREAKFAST BUSINESS THAT

25 EVENTUALLY CAME TO BE KNOWN AS R AND B LP.

26   MR. JESSUP-FRANKLIN:

27   I THINK YOU ARE GETTING INTO THE SENSITIVE AREA AND I WILL REMIND

[Document page 8]

1 MR. ROOKS TO REMEMBER OUR CONVERSATION.

2 THE WITNESS:

3 MR. DUPRIEST, I HAVE TO RESPECTFULLY DECLINE TO ANSWER THAT

4 QUESTION ON THE GROUNDS THAT ANY ANSWER I GIVE MAY HAVE A TENDENCY TO

5 INCRIMINATE ME.

6 BY MR. DUPRIEST:

7 Q MY QUESTION WAS NOT ABOUT THE BUSINESS BUT ABOUT YOUR KNOWLEDGE

8 AS TO WHETHER PASTOR YUN AND OTHERS WERE AWARE. WILL YOU ANSWER THAT

9 QUESTION?

10 A I DO NOT KNOW WHAT THEY WERE AWARE OF AND NOT AWARE OF.

11 Q DID YOU HAVE ANY OUTSIDE EMPLOYMENT OR OUTSIDE BUSINESS

12 ENTERPRISE DURING THE TIME YOU WORKED IN DR. NORTH'S PRACTICE?

13 A I MUST DECLINE TO ANSWER ON GROUNDS OF SELF-INCRIMINATION.

14 Q LET'S TALK ABOUT YOUR WORK AT BALD MOUNTAIN COMMUNITY CHURCH.

15 DID YOU WALK IN TO A FULLY DEVELOPED PRACTICE OR DID YOU HAVE TO BUILD

16 IT BY YOUR OWN EFFORTS?

17 A THE CHURCH HAS OPERATED A PASTORAL COUNSELING CENTER SINCE YR-

18 11. IT HAS BEEN REGULARLY STAFFED BY A FULLY QUALIFIED PASTORAL

19 COUNSELOR WHO IS AN ASSOCIATE PASTOR OF THE CHURCH AND SOMETIMES THERE

20 HAVE BEEN PART-TIME COUNSELORS AS WELL. THERE HAS BEEN ENOUGH WORK TO

21 KEEP THE PRACTICE BUSY ALMOST FROM THE BEGINNING. THE CHURCH WENT

22 THROUGH TWO OR THREE DIFFERENT PASTORAL COUNSELORS PRIOR TO MY

23 ARRIVAL. I KNOW THAT MY IMMEDIATE PREDECESSOR WAS LET GO BY THE CHURCH

24 IN JANUARY YR-03. THERE WAS SOME SORT OF SCANDAL BUT I DON'T KNOW THE

25 DETAILS. SO, BY THE TIME I ARRIVED, THE PASTORAL COUNSELING CENTER HAD

26 BEEN DORMANT FOR SIX MONTHS. THE PRIOR CLIENTS HAD ALL BEEN REFERRED

27 ELSEWHERE OR HAD SIMPLY SUSPENDED COUNSELING. MY ARRIVAL AT THE CHURCH

1 WAS ACCOMPANIED BY A FAIR AMOUNT OF PUBLICITY URGING PEOPLE TO AVAIL

2 THEMSELVES OF MY SERVICES. I PREACHED FOR THREE SUNDAYS IN A ROW SO

3 THAT THE CONGREGATION COULD BECOME FAMILIAR WITH ME. I ALSO GUEST

4 PREACHED AT A HALF A DOZEN OTHER CHURCHES IN THE COMMUNITY BECAUSE OUR

5 COUNSELING PROGRAM WELCOMES CLIENTS WHO ARE NOT MEMBERS OF OUR CHURCH.

6 BY THE TIME I HAD BEEN THERE SIX WEEKS, I HAD A FULL CLIENT LOAD AND

7 MORE SO, AND THAT WAS HOW IT WAS DURING MY ENTIRE TIME THERE.

8   Q   WAS ERNESTINE PETRILLO A CLIENT OF YOURS IN PASTORAL COUNSELING?

9   A   YES.

10   Q   WHEN DID YOU BEGIN COUNSELING HER?

11   A   IN MAY YR-02.

12   Q   DURING THE COURSE OF HER COUNSELING DID YOU ENCOURAGE HER TO

13 INVEST IN A LIMITED PARTNERSHIP OF WHICH YOU WERE A GENERAL PARTNER?

14   A   I MUST DECLINE TO ANSWER THAT QUESTION BOTH ON SELF-

15 INCRIMINATION GROUNDS AND BECAUSE IT INVOLVES CONFIDENTIAL

16 COMMUNICATIONS WITH A MEMBER OF THE CLERGY.

17   Q   IS THERE ANYTHING THAT YOU CAN SAY ABOUT MS. PETRILLO'S

18 COUNSELING RELATIONSHIP WITH YOU, YOUR CONDUCT IN RELATION TO HER, AND

19 HER CONDUCT IN RESPONSE TO YOUR COUNSELING?

20   A   OTHER THAN TO ACKNOWLEDGE THAT SHE WAS MY CLIENT AND RELEVANT

21 DATES, NO. I COULD ALSO TESTIFY ABOUT THE FEES SHE PAID, BUT IN THIS

22 CASE THERE WERE NONE BECAUSE THE CHURCH OFFERED THIS AS A FREE

23 SERVICE.

24   Q   DID YOU NOTICE CHANGES IN HER APPEARANCE OVER THE COURSE OF YOUR

25 COUNSELING OF HER? I AM NOT ASKING YOU TO REVEAL A CONFIDENTIAL

26 COMMUNICATION, ONLY TO RELATE WHAT YOU SAW.

27   A   I STAND ON MY PRIVILEGES, COUNSELOR.

[Document page 10]

1   Q   WOULD YOU TELL US ABOUT THE CIRCUMSTANCES OF BEING DISCHARGED

2 FROM YOUR MINISTRY AND COUNSELING SERVICE AT BALD MOUNTAIN COMMUNITY

3 CHURCH?

4   A   SOMETIME IN MAY YR-01, PASTOR YUN CAME TO ME AND SAID THAT

5 CERTAIN ACCUSATIONS HAD BEEN MADE. I AM NOT AT LIBERTY TO RELATE THE

6 ACCUSATIONS. SUFFICE IT TO SAY THAT I FELT I SHOULD TAKE AN IMMEDIATE

7 LEAVE OF ABSENCE UNTIL THIS MATTER COULD BE CLEARED UP. I KNOW THERE

8 WAS AN INVESTIGATION ALTHOUGH I DO NOT KNOW THE DETAILS. BY JULY

9 FIRST THE SITUATION HAD BECOME INTOLERABLE AND I RESIGNED.

10   Q   DID PASTOR YUN REQUEST YOUR RESIGNATION?

11   A   YES.

12   Q   YOU SUBSEQUENTLY FILED FOR BANKRUPTCY?

13   A   AN INVOLUNTARY BANKRUPTCY PETITION WAS FILED AGAINST ME IN MARCH

14 OF LAST YEAR.

15   Q   AND YOU ARE CURRENTLY FACING CRIMINAL CHARGES?

16   A   YES. THREE COUNTS OF ALLEGED VIOLATIONS OF THE ALABAMA

17 SECURITIES ACT.

18   Q   WOULD YOUR PLEASE DESCRIBE IN A GENERAL WAY THE ALLEGATIONS MADE

19 AGAINST YOU IN THE BANKRUPTCY PETITION AND THE CRIMINAL CHARGES?

20   MR. JESSUP-FRANKLIN:

21   THE COURT RECORDS ARE OPEN TO THE PUBLIC. YOU CAN GET THEM. BUT YOU

22 CAN'T FORCE MY CLIENT TO GIVE HIS VERSION OR HIS INTERPRETATION OF

23 THESE CHARGES. THAT'S INCRIMINATING AND I INSTRUCT REVEREND ROOKS NOT

24 TO ANSWER.

25   MR. DUPRIEST:

26   COUNSEL, YOU KNOW THAT YOU CANNOT ASSERT THE PRIVILEGE ON BEHALF OF

27 YOUR CLIENT, IT MUST BE ASSERTED BY YOUR CLIENT IN PERSON.

1   THE WITNESS:

2   I AM HERE IN PERSON AND I CLAIM THE PRIVILEGE. WILL THAT DO?

3   MR. DUPRIEST:

4   YES. I THINK THAT ABOUT DOES IT FOR US. MS. RUMSDALE, DO YOU WISH

5   TO INQUIRE?

6   MS. RUMSDALE:

7   I HAVE A FEW QUESTIONS, THANK YOU.

8   EXAMINATION ON BEHALF OF THE DEFENDANTS

9   BY MS. RUMSDALE:

10   Q   I WANT TO ASK YOU ABOUT PASTORAL COUNSELING IN GENERAL, AS

11   PRACTICED BY YOU, AND NOT ABOUT YOUR COUNSELING OF ANY PARTICULAR

12   CLIENT. OK?

13   A   OK.

14   Q   HOW DOES PASTORAL COUNSELING DIFFER FROM ANY OTHER FORM OF

15   COUNSELING?

16   A   SOME FORMS OF COUNSELING HAVE THE OBJECTIVE OF ASSISTING THE

17   CLIENT TO MAKE IMPORTANT LIFE DECISIONS. CAREER COUNSELING IS A GOOD

18   EXAMPLE. THE CLIENT WANTS HELP IN DECIDING WHAT CAREER PATHWAY TO

19   FOLLOW AND HOW TO GO ABOUT FOLLOWING IT. OTHER FORMS OF COUNSELING ARE

20   MORE RELATED TO THE PERSON AND ALL OF THE ISSUES AND PROBLEMS THAT A

21   PERSON MAY BE FACING IN ALL ASPECTS OF THEIR LIFE. ALL FORMS OF

22   COUNSELING USE TALK OR CONVERSATION TO HELP THE CLIENT CLARIFY THE

23   SITUATION AND UNDERSTAND THE CLIENT'S FEELINGS ABOUT THE SITUATION AND

24   HELP THE CLIENT TO BEHAVE EFFECTIVELY IN THE SITUATION IN ORDER TO

25   ACHIEVE THE CLIENT'S GOALS. PASTORAL COUNSELING IS GENERALLY LIKE

26   THAT. THE ONLY DIFFERENCE BETWEEN PASTORAL COUNSELING AND SECULAR

27   COUNSELING IS IN THE RELIGIOUS OR SPIRITUAL ORIENTATION OF PASTORAL

1   COUNSELING. THE CLIENT KNOWS THAT WHEN HE OR SHE COMES TO A PASTORAL

2   COUNSELOR, THE COUNSELOR WILL BE ABLE TO WORK WITH THE SPIRITUAL

3   DIMENSIONS OF THE CLIENT'S STRUGGLE, SOMETHING A SECULAR COUNSELOR MAY

4   NOT BE READY TO DO.

5   Q   HOW IMPORTANT IS THE RELIGIOUS OR SPIRITUAL DIMENSION OF

6   PASTORAL COUNSELING?

7   A   THE ANSWER DEPENDS ON BOTH THE COUNSELOR AND THE CLIENT. SOME

8   PASTORAL COUNSELORS YOU WATCH THEM IN ACTION AND YOU MIGHT NOT BE ABLE

9   TO TELL THAT THIS IS PASTORAL COUNSELING AS SUCH. OTHER PASTORAL

10 COUNSELORS BELIEVE THAT THE SPIRITUAL DIMENSION ALWAYS SHOULD BE

11 EMPHASIZED AND WILL USE RELIGIOUS SCRIPTURES AND IMAGERY ACTIVELY IN

12 THE PROCESS OF COUNSELING. AS FAR AS THE CLIENT IS CONCERNED, SOME

13 CLIENTS CLEARLY PERCEIVE THEIR PROBLEMS AS HAVING RELIGIOUS OR

14 SPIRITUAL DIMENSIONS, AND OTHERS DO NOT. SOME CLIENTS ENCOURAGE THE

15 COUNSELOR TO VISIT THE RELIGIOUS DIMENSION AND OTHERS DO NOT. SO IT

16 VARIES TREMENDOUSLY.

17   Q   WHAT IS YOUR PERSONAL VIEW OF THE RELIGIOUS OR SPIRITUAL

18 DIMENSION OF COUNSELING?

19   A   I DO NOT HAVE A FIXED VIEW OF THE RELIGIOUS DIMENSION AS SUCH.

20 IF THE CLIENT SEES THE PROBLEM AS A RELIGIOUS PROBLEM, I AM READY TO

21 ACCOMPANY THEM ON A RELIGIOUS JOURNEY. THE SPIRITUAL DIMENSION IS

22 ANOTHER MATTER. I BELIEVE THAT ALL PERSONAL PROBLEMS HAVE A SPIRITUAL

23 ASPECT, WHETHER YOU ARE TALKING ABOUT COUNSELING COUPLES WITH

24 DIFFICULTIES IN THEIR MARRIAGES, COUNSELING DEPRESSED PEOPLE WHO THINK

25 THEY SHOULD KILL THEMSELVES, COUNSELING TEENAGERS WHO ARE BEING

26 WOUNDED BY THE MEANNESS OF THEIR PEERS, COUNSELING MEN AND WOMEN ABOUT

27 ISSUES OF SEXUAL OR GENDER IDENTITY. YOU NAME IT. ALL OF THESE AREAS

1   OF CONCERN INVOLVE PEOPLE'S RELATIONSHIP TO THEIR SENSE OF HIGHER

2   PURPOSE AND A HIGHER POWER. EVEN IF NEITHER THE COUNSELOR NOR THE

3   CLIENT KNOWS IT, ALL COUNSELING AND ALL PSYCHOTHERAPY HAVE SPIRITUAL

4   DIMENSIONS.

5   Q   WHAT IS THE ROLE OF SCRIPTURES AND OTHER RELIGIOUS TEXTS?

6   A   A FEW COUNSELORS BELIEVE IN MOBILIZING THE AUTHORITY OF THE

7   SCRIPTURES TO ENCOURAGE PEOPLE TO ORGANIZE THEIR LIVES AS GOD INTENDS.

8   I DON'T BELIEVE IN USING SCRIPTURES AS AUTHORITY. I SEE THEM AS AN

9   INCREDIBLY RICH BODY OF LITERATURE THAT SPEAK IN WONDERFUL AND

10   POWERFUL WAYS TO PEOPLE OF ALL ERAS. I DON'T HAVE A PLAN FOR USING

11   SCRIPTURES IN COUNSELING, BUT WHEN AN IDEA SPONTANEOUSLY POPS INTO MY

12   MIND THAT CAN BE COMMUNICATED THROUGH A PASSAGE OF SCRIPTURE, I DO NOT

13   HESITATE TO BRING THE SCRIPTURE INTO THE CONVERSATION. PARTICULAR

14   PASSAGES CAN SOMETIMES BECOME THE THEME OF A WHOLE COURSE OF

15   COUNSELING OR CAN SERVE TO CHARACTERIZE PARTICULAR LIFE ISSUES THAT A

16   CLIENT FACES. YOU NAME A MENTAL, EMOTIONAL, OR PSYCHOLOGICAL PROBLEM

17   AND THERE ARE SCRIPTURAL PASSAGES THAT CAPTURE THEIR ESSENCE ONE WAY

18   OR ANOTHER. I TRY TO BE AWARE OF THESE CONNECTIONS AND GUIDE MY

19   CLIENTS TO RESONATING WITH THEM.

20   Q   HOW IMPORTANT IS RECREATION IN THE SPIRITUAL LIFE?

21   A   IT CAN BE IMPORTANT. HOW IMPORTANT DEPENDS.

22   Q   DO YOU ENCOURAGE YOUR CLIENTS TO ATTEND RELIGIOUS RETREATS?

23   A   SOMETIMES.

24   Q   WOULD A FACILITY THAT COMBINED FEATURES OF A RECREATIONAL

25   VACATION AND A RELIGIOUS RETREAT BE BENEFICIAL TO THE KINDS OF PEOPLE

26   THAT ARE SEEN IN PASTORAL COUNSELING?

27   A   THAT WAS VERY CLEVER, MS. RUMSDALE, BUT I AM NOT FALLING FOR IT.

[Document page 14]

1 YOU KNOW FULL WELL THAT ANY ANSWER I MIGHT GIVE COULD BECOME RELEVANT

2 EVIDENCE IN THE CRIMINAL CHARGES AGAINST ME. I MUST REFUSE TO ANSWER

3 ON GROUNDS OF SELF-INCRIMINATION

4   MS. RUMSDALE:

5   WELL I NEVER HEARD OF AN IDEA BEING INCRIMINATING, BUT I'LL LET IT

6 GO. NO FURTHER QUESTIONS.

7   THE REPORTER:

8   USUAL STIPULATIONS?

9   MR. DUPRIEST:

10   YES.

11   MS. RUMSDALE:

12   CERTAINLY.

13   (AT 11:03 A.M., MAY 20, YR-00, THE DEPOSITION OF LINWOOD ROOKS WAS

14 ADJOURNED.)

15 //

16 //

17 //

18 //

19 //

20 //

21 //

22 //

23 //

24 //

25 //

26 //

27 //

1   <u>REPORTER'S CERTIFICATE</u>

2   I, LEONARD AHERN, OFFICIAL COURT REPORTER OF THE STATE OF ALABAMA,

3 HEREBY CERTIFY THAT THE FOREGOING DEPOSITION OF LINWOOD ROOKS WAS

4 TAKEN BEFORE ME AT THE TIME AND PLACE HEREIN SET FORTH, AT WHICH TIME

5 THE WITNESS WAS PUT ON OATH BY ME;

6   THAT THE TESTIMONY OF THE WITNESS AND ALL OBJECTIONS MADE AT THE

7 TIME OF EXAMINATION WERE RECORDED STENOGRAPHICALLY BY ME, AND WERE

8 THEREAFTER TRANSCRIBED UNDER MY DIRECT SUPERVISION.

9   I FURTHER CERTIFY THAT I AM NEITHER COUNSEL FOR NOR RELATED TO ANY

10 PARTY TO SAID ACTION, NOR AM I IN ANYWISE INTERESTED IN THE OUTCOME

11 THEREOF.

12   IN WITNESS WHEREOF, I HAVE SUBSCRIBED MY NAME ON JUNE 2, YR-00.

Leonard Ahern

IN THE UNITED STATES DISTRICT COURT
FOR THE WESTERN DISTRICT OF ALABAMA

ERNESTINE PETRILLO

    PLAINTIFF

VS.

LINWOOD ROOKS, ET AL.

    DEFENDANTS

:
:
:
:
:
:
:
:
:
:

```
┌─────────────────────────────────────┐
│   UNITED STATES DISTRICT COURT       │
│             FILED                    │
│       June 4, YR-00                  │
│   WESTERN DISTRICT OF ALABAMA        │
└─────────────────────────────────────┘
```

CIVIL ACTION NO. 00-85FD

DEPOSITION OF HEATHER SEDALIA BURR

TAKEN BY PLAINTIFF AT 900 MAPLE LANE, BALD MOUNTAIN, ALABAMA,
COMMENCING AT 10:08 A.M., MAY 24, YR-00, BEFORE LEONARD AHERN,
CERTIFIED STENOGRAPHIC REPORTER.

APPEARANCES:

    FOR PLAINTIFF:

        WILSON & DUPRIEST

            BY: ARMAND DUPRIEST, ESQ.

        900 MAPLE LANE
        BALD MOUNTAIN, ALABAMA 36918
        TELEPHONE (934) 333-2541

    FOR DEFENDANTS HARRIETT YUN AND BALD MOUNTAIN COMMUNITY CHURCH:

        MILLER, ELDRIDGE & PASTERNAK

            BY: EMILY RUMSDALE, ESQ.

        13304 BALD MOUNTAIN PARKWAY
        BALD MOUNTAIN, ALABAMA 36918
        TELEPHONE (934) 485-9000

1   BALD MOUNTAIN, ALABAMA, MAY 24, YR-00

2   HEATHER SEDALIA BURR

3   HAVING BEEN DULY SWORN, TESTIFIED AS FOLLOWS:

4   EXAMINATION ON BEHALF OF THE PLAINTIFF

5   MR. DUPRIEST:

6   GOOD MORNING. MY NAME IS ARMAND DUPRIEST. I REPRESENT THE PLAINTIFF

7   IN THE CASE OF ERNESTINE PETRILLO VERSUS LINWOOD ROOKS, BALD MOUNTAIN

8   COMMUNITY CHURCH AND HARRIETT YUN, NO. 00-85 IN THE UNITED STATES

9   DISTRICT COURT FOR THE WESTERN DISTRICT OF ALABAMA. WE ARE HERE FOR

10   THE PREVIOUSLY-NOTICED DEPOSITION OF HEATHER SEDALIA BURR. ALSO

11   PRESENT TODAY ARE EMILY RUMSDALE, COUNSEL FOR THE DEFENDANTS COMMUNITY

12   CHURCH AND HARRIETT YUN, AND OUR EVER-FAITHFUL COURT REPORTER, LEONARD

13   AHERN. IF THERE ARE NO PRELIMINARY MATTERS, LET'S GET STARTED.

14   BY MR. DUPRIEST:

15   Q   MS. BURR, WOULD YOU PLEASE STATE AND SPELL YOUR NAME FOR THE

16   RECORD?

17   A   MY NAME IS HEATHER H-E-A-T-H-E-R SEDALIA S-E-D-A-L-I-A BURR

18   THAT'S B-U-R-R.

19   [PRELIMINARY QUESTIONS. SEE FOOTNOTE 4, PAGE 60, SUPRA.]

20   * * *

21   Q   WHERE DO YOU LIVE?

22   A   I LIVE IN CINCINNATI, OHIO.

23   Q   WHAT IS YOUR OCCUPATION?

24   A   I AM A METHODIST MINISTER AND PASTOR OF ST. ANDREWS UNITED

25   METHODIST CHURCH IN CINCINNATI.

26   Q   ARE YOU ACQUAINTED WITH ANY OF THE INDIVIDUAL PARTIES TO THIS

27   LITIGATION, ERNESTINE PETRILLO, LINWOOD ROOKS, AND HARRIETT YUN OR

1 WITH EITHER OF THE LAWYERS, MYSELF, ARMAND DUPRIEST, AND COUNSEL FOR

2 THE DEFENDANTS MS. EMILY RUMSDALE?

3   A   I DON'T KNOW ERNESTINE PETRILLO, I KNOW LINWOOD ROOKS VERY WELL,

4 I BELIEVE I HAVE MET HARRIETT YUN BUT AM NOT CLOSELY ACQUAINTED WITH

5 HER, AND I MET YOU AND MS. RUMSDALE FOR THE FIRST TIME THIS MORNING.

6   Q   WHEN DID YOU FIRST MEET LINWOOD ROOKS?

7   A   IT WAS AROUND CHRISTMAS YR-06.

8   Q   HOW DID YOU MEET HIM?

9   A   IT WAS AT A SMALL RECEPTION FOR AN ORGANIZATION OF PROTESTANT

10 MINISTERS TO WHICH I BELONG IN CINCINNATI. MR. ROOKS WAS A GUEST AT

11 THE RECEPTION. WE FELL INTO CONVERSATION AND FOUND THAT WE SHARED MANY

12 INTERESTS AND VALUES. WE SOON BECAME CLOSE FRIENDS.

13   Q   WHAT DID YOU HAVE IN COMMON?

14   A   OH, AN INTEREST IN CERTAIN THEOLOGICAL WRITERS, AN INTEREST IN

15 PASTORAL COUNSELING, AN INTEREST IN NFL FOOTBALL, AND A SHARED BELIEF

16 THAT MINISTERS ARE UNDERPAID AND IT'S THEIR OWN FAULT.

17   Q   ARE YOU A PASTORAL COUNSELOR?

18   A   I HAVE HAD SOME TRAINING IN COUNSELING AND I DO A BIT OF

19 COUNSELING IN MY PASTORAL ROLE, BUT I AM NOT A FULL-TIME PASTORAL

20 COUNSELOR NOR DO I HOLD MYSELF OUT AS A SPECIALIST. MOST MINISTERS DO

21 A CERTAIN AMOUNT OF WHAT YOU WOULD CALL COUNSELING IN THEIR EVERYDAY

22 WORK WITH INDIVIDUAL MEMBERS OF THE CONGREGATION. WHEN IT BECOMES

23 MORE FORMALIZED WE GIVE IT THE FANCY TITLE PASTORAL COUNSELING, BUT

24 MOST OF US DO IT QUITE INFORMALLY AND WITHOUT ANY FANFARE.

25   Q   TELL ME ABOUT THE IDEA THAT MINISTERS ARE UNDERPAID AND WHY YOU

26 THINK IT'S THEIR OWN FAULT?

27   A   WELL IT'S NO SECRET THAT THE COMPENSATION THAT MOST CHURCHES AND

1   CONGREGATIONS CAN AFFORD TO PAY THEIR CLERGY IS WOEFULLY LOW. THAT

2   FACT HAS SEVERAL CONSEQUENCES. ONE IS THAT CLERGY ARE INVITED TO

3   BELIEVE THAT THEIR HOLY CALLING IS ENOUGH OF A REWARD IN ITSELF. BUT

4   EXCEPT FOR CLOISTERED RELIGIOUS PERSONS, CLERGY HAVE TO LIVE IN THIS

5   WORLD. THEY HAVE TO EAT. THEY HAVE TO EDUCATE THEIR KIDS. AND SO

6   FORTH. THERE ARE MANY PERQUISITES THAT CLERGY ENJOY THAT ARE DESIGNED

7   TO LOWER THEIR EXPENSES OR INCREASE THEIR INCOME. SOME OF THESE ARE

8   FRANKLY DEMEANING TO CLERGY AND THEIR FAMILIES. I COULD GO ON, BUT I

9   HOPE THAT'S ENOUGH FOR YOU TO GET THE PICTURE. MANY CLERGY ARE FORCED

10 TO WORK SECOND JOBS, BUT THIS CAN BE A PROBLEM FOR BOTH THE MINISTER

11 AND THE CONGREGATION IF THE CONGREGATION BELIEVES THAT IT HAS CALLED A

12 FULL-TIME MINISTER. MANY CLERGY BUILD AT-HOME BUSINESSES, SUCH AS

13 AMWAY. LINWOOD AND I SPENT LONG HOURS TALKING ABOUT THE ECONOMICS OF

14 THE MINISTRY, AND ONE THING WE QUICKLY AGREED ON IS THAT PLANS FOR

15 SUPPLEMENTING THE INCOME OF CLERGY WOULD BE MOST SUCCESSFUL IF THEY

16 BUILT ON THE KINDS OF TALENTS THAT CLERGY PEOPLE OFTEN POSSESS. THERE

17 ARE A FEW WELL-KNOWN EXAMPLES. A FEW CLERGY HAVE BECOME NATIONALLY

18 PROMINENT BY WRITING AND PUBLISHING RELIGIOUS BOOKS. SOME OF THEM HAVE

19 BECOME QUITE WEALTHY. NORMAN VINCENT PEALE COMES TO MIND AS AN EARLY

20 EXAMPLE. MANY CLERGY ARE INSPIRATIONAL SPEAKERS. SOME CLERGY MAKE

21 THEMSELVES AVAILABLE AS MOTIVATIONAL SPEAKERS TO COMMUNITY GROUPS,

22 CORPORATE GROUPS, EMPLOYEE GROUPS. THERE ARE GOOD FEES TO BE EARNED. A

23 WELL-KNOWN MOTIVATIONAL SPEAKER CAN WORK FIVE TO TEN HOURS PER WEEK

24 AND EARN MORE THAN TRIPLE THEIR MINISTERIAL SALARIES.

25   Q   ARE THESE THE IDEAS THAT LED TO THE CONCEPT OF RELIGIOUS OR

26 SPIRITUAL BED AND BREAKFAST INNS?

27   A   EXACTLY. LINWOOD AND I BRAINSTORMED EXTENSIVELY AND CAME TO

REALIZE THAT THERE ARE MANY RELIGIOUS PEOPLE WHOSE NEED OR DESIRE FOR

SPIRITUAL NURTURANCE EXTENDS BEYOND THEIR ACTIVITY AS CHURCH MEMBERS.

WE ALSO REALIZED THAT SPIRITUAL NEEDS AND RECREATIONAL NEEDS THAT

PEOPLE HAVE TO RECHARGE THEMSELVES FOR THEIR DAILY LIVES ARE NOT ALL

THAT DIFFERENT. THERE ARE MANY WELL-TO-DO PEOPLE WHO SET LIMITS ON THE

AMOUNTS THEY ARE WILLING TO GIVE TO CHURCHES AND CHURCH ORGANIZATIONS,

BUT WHO HAVE MUCH MORE LIBERAL ATTITUDES TOWARDS THE AMOUNTS THEY ARE

WILLING TO SPEND ON THEMSELVES. LINWOOD AND I TALKED TO MANY PEOPLE

ABOUT HOW MUCH TIME THEY SPEND ON VACATIONS AND OTHER FORMS OF

RECREATION, HOW MUCH THEY DEVOTE TO MAINTAINING THEIR SPIRITUALITY,

AND WE LEARNED THAT MANY PEOPLE FEEL THERE IS A DISPROPORTION IN THEIR

LIVES. THESE DISCUSSIONS MATURED INTO RATHER CAREFUL MARKETING

STUDIES, THOUGH WE HAD TO DO THEM ON THE CHEAP. BUT I WAS ORIGINALLY

TRAINED IN MARKETING, AND I WAS ABLE TO COLLECT A GREAT DEAL OF

INFORMATION THAT EVENTUALLY LED US TO THE SPIRITUALLY ORIENTED BED AND

BREAKFAST BUSINESS.

Q   CAN YOU SAY MORE ABOUT THE CONCEPT?

A   WE WOULD ACQUIRE PROPERTIES THAT COULD BE OR HAD BEEN OPERATED

SUCCESSFULLY AS BED AND BREAKFAST INNS IN POPULAR VACATION AND TOURIST

DESTINATIONS. THE INNS WOULD BE LIKE OTHER B AND B EXPERIENCES EXCEPT

WE WOULD ADD A SPIRITUAL COMPONENT. THE HOST AND HOSTESSES WOULD BE

SPIRITUALLY TRAINED PERSONS, MOST OF THEM CLERGY. A DAILY PROGRAM OF

PRAYER, MEDITATION, BIBLE STUDIES, AND OTHER KINDS OF ACTIVITIES WOULD

BE CONDUCTED AT THE INN. CONVERSATION AROUND THE BREAKFAST TABLE OR IN

THE EVENING IN THE LIVING ROOM WOULD BE GENTLY GUIDED AWAY FROM

MUNDANE TOPICS TOWARDS MORE MEANINGFUL TOPICS. WE DEVELOPED SEVERAL

PROTOCOLS FOR TYPICAL DAYS AT ONE OF OUR INNS. WE ALSO MADE A PLAN FOR

[Document page 5]

1   SPECIAL OCCASIONS THAT WOULD BE LIKE A FULL-BLOWN RELIGIOUS RETREAT.

2   BOTH OF US HAD ATTENDED RELIGIOUS RETREATS AND WE HAD GOOD IDEAS ABOUT

3   HOW TO BORROW AND APPLY THE BEST OF WHAT WE HAD EXPERIENCED. WE WERE

4   AWARE THAT MANY PEOPLE ARE JEALOUS OF THEIR VACATION TIME AND WOULD BE

5   RELUCTANT TO GIVE UP NORMAL VACATION ACTIVITIES. SO WE CONCEIVED OF

6   LOCATING OUR INNS IN AREAS WITH GOOD RECREATIONAL OPPORTUNITIES. NEAR

7   NATIONAL PARKS OR THE OCEAN OR FAMOUS HISTORICAL SITES. I COULD GO

8   INTO MORE DETAIL, IF YOU LIKE, OR I COULD GIVE YOU A COPY OF OUR

9   DEVELOPMENT PLAN AND OF OUR BUSINESS PLAN, WHICH GO INTO MUCH MORE

10 DETAIL.

11   MR. DUPRIEST:

12   THANK YOU. IF YOU COULD MAIL ONE EACH OF THOSE TO ME AND MS.

13 RUMSDALE, THAT WOULD BE VERY GOOD OF YOU. THEY MAY RAISE SOME

14 ADDITIONAL QUESTIONS AND WE COULD ARRANGE A CONVENIENT WAY FOR YOU TO

15 GIVE SUPPLEMENTAL TESTIMONY IN WRITING AND NOT HAVE TO TRAVEL ALL THE

16 WAY DOWN HERE AGAIN.

17   BY MR. DUPRIEST:

18   Q   WHAT WAS THE BASIC PLAN FOR SECURING CAPITAL FINANCING?

19   A   WE RAISED SOME SEED MONEY AMONG FRIENDS AND ACQUAINTANCES AS

20 WELL AS FROM A VENTURE CAPITAL FIRM THAT HAPPENS TO BE HEADED BY A

21 VERY RELIGIOUS PERSON WITH WHOM WE SHARED OUR IDEA. THAT SEED MONEY

22 WAS ENOUGH TO INDUCE TWO DIFFERENT COMMERCIAL LENDERS TO BACK OUR PLAN

23 WITH SUBSTANTIAL LOANS. WE HAD A PLAN FOR A PHASED ACQUISITION OF

24 PROPERTIES, CONVERSION OF THE PROPERTIES TO OUR KIND OF OPERATION, AND

25 ACTUAL OPERATION OF THE PROPERTIES ALONG THE LINES OF OUR CONCEPT. WE

26 REALIZED WE WOULD HAVE TO HAVE ONE FULL-TIME HOST AT EACH PROPERTY AND

27 ADDITIONAL WORKERS SUCH AS CHAMBER MAIDS, GARDENERS, AND THE LIKE. BUT

1　WE ALSO REALIZED THAT WE COULD OFFER DISCOUNTED ACCOMMODATIONS TO

2　MEMBERS OF THE CLERGY WHO WOULD TAKE OUR BRIEF TRAINING COURSE, AND

3　THEY WOULD BECOME ACTIVE PARTICIPANTS IN THE DAILY PROGRAMS OF PRAYER,

4　MEDITATION, BIBLE STUDIES, DISCUSSION GROUPS, AND THE LIKE. WE LAID

5　OUT ON A TIME LINE WHEN WE WOULD ACQUIRE EACH INN, HOW EACH INN WOULD

6　BE BROUGHT TO PROFITABILITY ENABLING US TO ACQUIRE THE NEXT INN, AND

7　SO FORTH.

8　Q　WHERE DID THE LIMITED PARTNERSHIP FIT IN?

9　A　WE NEEDED NOT ONLY TO BORROW MONEY, WHICH WE WOULD REPAY, BUT WE

10　NEEDED EQUITY INVESTORS. WITH THE HELP OF A VERY GRACIOUS LAW FIRM

11　THAT DONATED ITS TIME, WE CREATED A LIMITED PARTNERSHIP STRUCTURE,

12　WITH LINWOOD AND ME AS THE GENERAL PARTNERS.　WE WOULD SELL LIMITED

13　PARTNERSHIP INTERESTS FOR TWO THOUSAND DOLLARS EACH, AND WE EXPECTED

14　AT THE END OF TWO YEARS THAT WE SHOULD BE ABLE TO ATTRACT AT LEAST TWO

15　MILLION DOLLARS OF EQUITY INVESTMENT.

16　Q　DID YOU EVER BEGIN OPERATING A BED AND BREAKFAST INN ALONG THESE

17　LINES?

18　A　OH, YES.

19　Q　HELP ME UNDERSTAND THE SEQUENCE OF EVENTS. WHEN DID YOU AND MR.

20　ROOKS FIRST START DISCUSSING THE BED AND BREAKFAST IDEA.

21　A　NOT LONG AFTER WE MET IN YR-06.　BY EARLY YR-05 OUR PLANS WERE

22　FAR ENOUGH ALONG THAT WE SET UP THE LIMITED PARTNERSHIP STRUCTURE AND

23　ALSO SECURED OUR FIRST LOANS.　SHALL I GO ON?

24　Q　PLEASE.

25　A　IN YR-04 WE PURCHASED TWO PROPERTIES, ONE IN FLORIDA AND ONE IN

26　MICHIGAN, AND WE HIRED ARCHITECTS AND CONTRACTORS TO REMODEL THOSE

27　PROPERTIES, WHICH THEY WERE ABLE TO DO ON A VERY SHORT TIMETABLE.　I

1   TOOK A LEAVE OF ABSENCE FROM MY REGULAR MINISTRY, AND MOVED TO

2   MICHIGAN TO OPERATE THAT PROPERTY FOR THE FIRST FEW MONTHS. WE OPENED

3   FOR BUSINESS ON JANUARY 15, YR-03. WE HIRED A FULL-TIME HOST FOR THE

4   FLORIDA PROPERTY AND ALSO SET UP ARRANGEMENTS WITH A NETWORK OF PEOPLE

5   TO HELP SUPPLEMENT THE HOST'S CONTRIBUTIONS TO THE SPIRITUAL PROGRAMS.

6   WE OPENED THE FLORIDA PROPERTY IN JUNE YR-03. WE HAD PLANS FOR

7   ACQUIRING TWO MORE PROPERTIES TOWARDS THE END OF YR-03, BUT THAT NEVER

8   WORKED OUT.

9   Q   WHY NOT?

10   A   WE WERE NEVER ABLE TO OPERATE IN THE BLACK. BOTH PROPERTIES

11   BEGAN LOSING MONEY AS SOON AS WE OPENED THEM.

12   Q   TO WHAT DO YOU ATTRIBUTE THAT?

13   A   GENERAL ECONOMIC CONDITIONS FOR ONE THING. SECOND, IN RETROSPECT

14   I BELIEVE THAT OUR MARKETING PLAN WAS EXTREMELY WEAK. WE JUST DID NOT

15   GET OUT AND SELL OURSELVES TO POTENTIAL CUSTOMERS IN TIME TO START THE

16   REVENUE FLOWING. OUR OCCUPANCY RATES WERE AROUND 20 PERCENT, WHEREAS

17   WE HAD PLANNED ON THE BASIS OF 80 PERCENT. OF COURSE WE WOULD HAVE

18   GOOD WEEKS AROUND HOLIDAYS, AND THE LIKE, BUT WE JUST DID NOT ATTRACT

19   THE BUSINESS WE THOUGHT WAS THERE.

20   Q   DID YOU REPORT THESE LOSSES TO YOUR INVESTORS?

21   A   YES WE DID. OUR END OF THE YEAR REPORT FOR YR-03 PAINTED A

22   GLOOMY PICTURE. WHEN THAT WAS ISSUED, IT BECAME ALMOST IMPOSSIBLE TO

23   ATTRACT NEW INVESTORS. WE DID EVERYTHING WE COULD TO BOOST PATRONAGE,

24   TO CUT COSTS, BUT WE JUST DID NOT HAVE ENOUGH TO WORK WITH. WE BEGAN

25   DIPPING INTO CAPITAL TO PAY FOR ORDINARY EXPENSES. IN JANUARY YR-01,

26   WE SUSPENDED PAYMENTS TO OUR CREDITORS. WE HOPED THAT WOULD BE

27   TEMPORARY, BUT WE NEVER RESUMED PAYING OUR CREDITORS. FINALLY, IN

[Document page 8]

MARCH YR-01 WE HAD A PETITION FOR BANKRUPTCY FILED AGAINST US. THE
BANKRUPTCY TRUSTEE IMMEDIATELY SHUT DOWN THE INNS AND BEGAN SELLING
OFF OUR ASSETS, AND THE REST IS HISTORY.

Q   AS GENERAL PARTNERS, HOW DID YOU AND MR. ROOKS DIVIDE UP YOUR
RESPONSIBILITIES?

A   I WAS PRIMARILY RESPONSIBLE FOR FINANCES AND MARKETING. MR.
ROOKS WAS PRIMARILY RESPONSIBLE FOR PROGRAM DEVELOPMENT AND
OPERATIONS.

Q   DID THE COMPANY HAVE AN OFFICE, HEADQUARTERS, ANYTHING LIKE
THAT?

A   WE PRETTY MUCH OPERATED OUT OF OUR HOMES IN CINCINNATI. WHEN
LINWOOD MOVED TO ALABAMA WE DECIDED TO REORGANIZE THE BUSINESS AS A
LIMITED PARTNERSHIP UNDER ALABAMA LAW. AT THAT TIME WE OPENED A SMALL
OFFICE WITH ONE PART-TIME EMPLOYEE. THE LIMITED PARTNERSHIP AGREEMENT
WAS SET UP UNDER ALABAMA LAW AND DECLARED THAT ALABAMA WOULD BE OUR
PRINCIPAL PLACE OF BUSINESS

Q   WERE THE LIMITED PARTNERSHIP INTERESTS REGISTERED AS SECURITIES
WITH THE ALABAMA SECURITIES COMMISSION?

A   NO, THEY WEREN'T. WE NEVER WERE TOLD THAT WAS REQUIRED AND WE
DIDN'T THINK ABOUT.

Q   DIDN'T YOUR LAWYERS ADVISE YOU?

A   NO. I GUESS THAT'S ONE OF THE RISKS OF RELYING ON VOLUNTEERS.

Q   YOU SAY YOU WERE PRIMARILY IN CHARGE OF FINANCES AND MARKETING.
TO WHAT EXTENT DID YOU KEEP MR. ROOKS ADVISED OF OCCURRENCES IN THE
FINANCIAL AREA?

A   WE TALKED ALMOST EVERY DAY ON THE TELEPHONE. I ALWAYS GAVE HIM A
DAILY REPORT AND HE GAVE ME A REPORT ON WHAT WAS HAPPENING IN HIS

[Document page 9]

1   AREA. I WOULD SAY THAT EACH OF US WAS FULLY APPRISED OF EVERYTHING

2   THAT WAS GOING ON.

3   Q   HOW WERE LIMITED PARTNERSHIP INTERESTS SOLD?

4   A   EACH OF US SOLD LIMITED PARTNERSHIP INTERESTS WHENEVER WE COULD.

5   WE EACH HAD COPIES OF THE LEAFLETS THAT WE USED TO EXPLAIN THE

6   BUSINESS, AND BOTH OF US HAD A SUPPLY OF THE CERTIFICATES. WHENEVER

7   ONE OF US SOLD SHARES, THEY WOULD ISSUE A CERTIFICATE AND ENTER

8   INFORMATION ON THE NEW LIMITED PARTNERSHIP ON THE BOOKS.

9   Q   HOW WERE THE BOOKS KEPT?

10   A   WE USED A COMPUTERIZED BOOK-KEEPING SYSTEM THAT EACH OF US COULD

11 ACCESS VIA A SECURE SITE ON THE WEB.

12   Q   WHO SIGNED THE CERTIFICATES OF LIMITED PARTNERSHIP INTERESTS?

13   A   WE DECIDED TO KEEP IT SIMPLE AND HAVE ONE PERSON SIGN ALL OF

14 THOSE CERTIFICATES. SINCE I WAS SUPPOSEDLY THE FINANCIAL GURU, THAT

15 TASK FELL TO ME. BUT LINWOOD KEPT A SUPPLY OF SIGNED CERTIFICATES FOR

16 HIS USE WHENEVER HE WOULD MAKE A SALE.

17   Q   DID ANYONE EVER COMPLAIN ABOUT YOUR ACTIVITIES IN SELLING THESE

18 LIMITED PARTNERSHIP INTERESTS?

19   A   WELL THE SECURITIES COMMISSION CAME VISITING IN EARLY YR-01, AND

20 THAT'S WHEN I LEARNED HOW MESSED UP THAT SIDE OF THE BUSINESS WAS.

21   Q   DID EITHER ONE OF YOU EVER ATTEMPT TO SELL LIMITED PARTNERSHIP

22 INTERESTS DURING THE COURSE OF YOUR REGULAR JOBS. THAT IS, DID YOU TRY

23 TO SELL TO MEMBERS OF YOUR CHURCH OR DID MR. ROOKS TRY TO SELL TO

24 CLIENTS OF HIS COUNSELING PRACTICE?

25   A   I WOULD SELL A FEW SHARES TO PARISHIONERS THAT I THOUGHT WOULD

26 BE INTERESTED, BUT I DID NOT MAKE A BIG PUSH. I GATHER THAT LINWOOD

27 TRIED TO SELL SHARES TO HIS COUNSELING CLIENTS BECAUSE HE TOLD ME ONE

TIME THAT HIS BOSS HAD TOLD HIM NOT TO DO THAT.

Q   DID LINWOOD STOP THAT ACTIVITY?

A   I'M NOT SURE. I KNOW THAT A COUPLE OF TIMES HE SOLD A FEW SHARES AND ENTERED THEM ON THE BOOKS AND I ASKED HIM "WHO'S JOHN SMITH," OR WHATEVER THE NAME WAS, AND HE TOLD ME IT WAS ONE OF HIS COUNSELING CLIENTS.

Q   HOW DID YOU REACT TO THAT?

A   NO REACTION. AS LONG AS LINWOOD WAS NOT BREAKING THE LAW I FIGURED THAT I HAD NO BUSINESS TRYING TO MICRO MANAGE HIS SELLING ACTIVITIES.

Q   BUT WHAT ABOUT THE FACT THAT HIS BOSS HAD TOLD HIM NOT TO DO THAT?

A   THAT WAS LINWOOD'S PROBLEM, NOT MINE.

Q   DO YOU RECALL WHEN LINWOOD TOLD YOU HIS BOSS HAD TOLD HIM TO STOP SELLING SHARES TO CLIENTS?

A   OH, I THINK IT WAS SOMETIME IN THE SPRING OF YR-04.

Q   AND WHEN DID LINWOOD REPORT THE SALE OF THE INTERESTS THAT YOU JUST MENTIONED WHERE YOU ASKED HIM WHO JOHN SMITH WAS?

A   I THINK THAT WAS ONLY A WEEK OR TWO BEFORE LINWOOD LEFT TO TAKE THE POSITION IN BALD MOUNTAIN.

Q   WOULD JUNE OR JULY YR-03 SEEM APPROXIMATELY CORRECT AS AN ESTIMATE OF WHEN?

A   THAT SEEMS ABOUT RIGHT.

Q   WHAT DO YOU RECALL ABOUT A LIMITED PARTNER NAMED ERNESTINE PETRILLO?

A   THERE WERE TWO INSTANCES IN YR-02 WHEN LINWOOD SOLD SHARES IN THE LIMITED PARTNERSHIP WITHOUT TELLING ME. WE HAD AGREED IN JUNE YR-

1 02 TO STOP SELLING THE SHARES. I THINK WE REALIZED AT THAT TIME THAT

2 THE BUSINESS WAS DOOMED AND IT WOULD NOT BE WISE TO SELL ANY MORE

3 SHARES. WELL, SOMETIME RIGHT AFTER THAT I NOTICED ON THE BOOKS A NEW

4 LIMITED PARTNER WHO HAD PURCHASED TEN THOUSAND DOLLARS WORTH OF SHARES

5 IN SEPTEMBER YR-02.

6   Q   WAS THAT MS. PETRILLO?

7   A   NO. IT WAS SOMEONE ELSE. A MALE, I BELIEVE. I CAN'T REMEMBER

8 HIS NAME.

9   Q   WOULD YOU HAVE ANY WAY OF REFRESHING YOUR RECOLLECTION?

10   A   HIS NAME IS ENTERED IN THE WEB BASED BOOKKEEPING SYSTEM THAT WE

11 USED, BUT THE BANKRUPTCY TRUSTEE HAS CONTROL OF THAT. MY PASSWORD HAS

12 BEEN CANCELED AND THERE'S NO WAY I COULD ACCESS THAT INFORMATION.

13   Q   COULD YOU REQUEST THAT INFORMATION FROM THE BANKRUPTCY TRUSTEE?

14   A   I SUPPOSE I COULD ASK FOR THE MOON OR A GLASS OF WATER, BUT I AM

15 NOT GOING TO. MY RELATIONSHIP WITH THE BANKRUPTCY TRUSTEE IS NOT

16 EXACTLY CORDIAL.

17   Q   SO THE MAN WHOSE NAME YOU DO NOT REMEMBER PURCHASED SHARES IN

18 SEPTEMBER YR-02. DID HE PAY FOR THEM?

19   A   I DON'T REMEMBER RECEIVING HIS PAYMENT. IF HE HAD NOT PAID I

20 THINK I WOULD REMEMBER THAT. BUT I REALLY DON'T KNOW.

21   Q   WHAT ABOUT THE SHARES HE SOLD TO MS. PETRILLO?

22   A   THE FIRST PURCHASE WAS RECORDED IN OCTOBER YR-02. IT WAS FOR

23 TWO SHARES AT TWO THOUSAND DOLLARS. TWO MONTHS LATER, HE RECORDED THE

24 SALE OF 64 SHARES TO MS. PETRILLO. I WAS THUNDERSTRUCK. THAT'S $128

25 THOUSAND WORTH OF LIMITED PARTNERSHIP INTERESTS.

26   Q   HOW DID MS. PETRILLO PAY FOR THOSE SHARES?

27   A   CASHIER'S CHECKS FROM A BANK.

1   Q   DID YOU EVER HAVE DIRECT CONTACT WITH MS. PETRILLO?

2   A   NO.

3   Q   DID YOU EVER HAVE TELEPHONE CONTACT WITH HER?

4   A   NOT THAT I RECALL.

5   Q   MS. PETRILLO TESTIFIED IN HER DEPOSITION THAT SHE TELEPHONED YOU

6   PRIOR TO EACH OF HER PURCHASES OF LIMITED PARTNERSHIP INTERESTS. DOES

7   THAT JIBE WITH YOUR RECOLLECTION?

8   A   IT'S POSSIBLE PRIOR TO THE FIRST PURCHASE, SHE CALLED AND WE

9   DISCUSSED THE COMPANY AND THE NATURE OF THE INVESTMENT. I RECEIVED A

10   LOT OF CALLS LIKE THAT AND MAYBE I JUST HAVE NOT HOOKED THAT UP IN MY

11   MIND WITH THE PERSON TO WHOM THOSE FINAL SHARES WERE SOLD. BUT I AM

12   SURE I WOULD REMEMBER A SECOND CALL FROM HER. BY THEN SHE WAS ALREADY

13   AN INVESTOR AND I WOULD REMEMBER. AND ALSO HER SECOND PURCHASE WAS

14   VERY LARGE. I WOULD REMEMBER TALKING TO HER ABOUT THAT PURCHASE, AND

15   I AM SURE I DID NOT.

16   Q   DID YOU DO ANYTHING IN RESPONSE TO EITHER OF MS. PETRILLO'S

17   PURCHASES?

18   A   WELL, OF COURSE, I WOULD HAVE MADE ENTRIES IN THE CAPITAL

19   ACCOUNT OF OUR COMPUTERIZED BOOKS, THOUGH LINWOOD MAY HAVE TAKEN CARE

20   OF THAT. I DON'T REMEMBER. AND I KNOW I SENT LINWOOD AN E-MAIL AFTER

21   THE SECOND PURCHASE. I SAID I HOPE YOU KNOW WHAT YOU ARE DOING AND I

22   HOPE YOU TOLD THIS WOMAN THE TRUTH ABOUT THE BUSINESS. HE SAID, DON'T

23   WORRY ABOUT IT.

24   Q   IS THAT ALL HE SAID, DON'T WORRY?

25   A   THAT'S ALL.

26   Q   DIDN'T THAT SET OFF ANY ALARMS IN YOU?

27   A   IT SHOULD HAVE. BUT I WAS SO SHELL SHOCKED AT THAT TIME, BECAUSE

[Document page 13]

1 I KNEW THE BUSINESS HAD ALREADY FAILED AND IT WAS JUST A MATTER OF

2 TIME. I FIGURED WHATEVER LINWOOD WANTED TO DO, HE COULD DO IT, AND IT

3 WASN'T MY CONCERN. I DID NOT REALIZE AT THAT TIME THAT I COULD GET IN

4 TROUBLE ON ACCOUNT OF HIS ACTIONS.

5   Q DID YOU GET IN TROUBLE?

6   A APART FROM LOSING THE BUSINESS AND ALL OF MY INVESTMENT, NO. I

7 HAVE BEEN INTERVIEWED EXTENSIVELY BY INVESTIGATORS FOR THE ALABAMA

8 SECURITIES COMMISSION AND I AM AWARE THAT I COULD BE CHARGED FOR

9 VIOLATING THAT LAW. HOWEVER, I BELIEVE THAT MY COOPERATION WITH THEIR

10 INVESTIGATION MAY BE WORTH SOMETHING.

11   Q HAVE YOU BEEN GRANTED IMMUNITY?

12   A NOT YET.

13   Q ARE YOU EXPECTING TO BE GRANTED IMMUNITY?

14   A WELL, I AM HOPEFUL.

15   Q WHAT HAVE THE SECURITIES INVESTIGATORS SAID TO YOU ABOUT THE

16 PROSPECT OF IMMUNITY?

17   A JUST THAT IT IS A POSSIBILITY BUT THAT HOW I FARE WILL DEPEND ON

18 MY BEING TOTALLY FORTHCOMING AND TRUTHFUL IN THE INVESTIGATION.

19 BY MR. DUPRIEST:

20 THANK YOU REVEREND BURR. YOUR WITNESS.

21   EXAMINATION ON BEHALF OF THE DEFENDANTS

22 BY MS. RUMSDALE:

23   Q WHAT IS YOUR ATTITUDE TOWARDS REVEREND ROOKS AT THIS TIME?

24   A I STILL CARE FOR LINWOOD VERY MUCH. HE WAS A VERY GOOD FRIEND. I

25 WAS DISAPPOINTED BY SOME OF HIS ACTIONS, BUT I WAS ALSO DISAPPOINTED

26 BY SOME OF MY OWN ACTIONS. THERE'S ENOUGH BLAME TO GO AROUND. I HAVE

27 COMPLETELY AND WITHOUT RESERVATION FORGIVEN LINWOOD FOR ALL THE

GRIEVANCES THAT I MIGHT HAVE HAD AGAINST HIM.

Q   HOW MUCH HAVE YOU SEEN EACH OTHER IN THE PAST YEAR?

A   I HAVE SEEN VERY LITTLE OF LINWOOD SINCE THE BANKRUPTCY WAS FILED. HE CALLED ME WHEN HE WAS CHARGED WITH CRIMINAL VIOLATIONS OF THE SECURITIES ACT. HE SAID HE WAS SORRY BUT HIS LAWYERS HAD INSTRUCTED HIM TO HAVE NO CONTACT WITH ME. WE MADE OUR GOOD-BYES AND I HAVE NOT HEARD FROM HIM SINCE.

Q   I ASSUME THAT YOU ARE ANGRY AT LINWOOD FOR ALL THE GRIEF HE CAUSED YOU?

A   NOT SO.

Q   IF YOU LOOK DEEP IN YOUR HEART, DO YOU SEE THERE AT LEAST SOME HINT OF A DESIRE TO GET EVEN WITH HIM?

A   NOT AT ALL. I TOLD YOU I HAVE FORGIVEN HIM. TO ME, FORGIVENESS IS NOT SOMETHING I TURN ON AND OFF. ONCE I FORGIVE, THE GRIEVANCE DISAPPEARS.

Q   YOU PREVIOUSLY TESTIFIED ABOUT MR. ROOKS INFORMING YOU ABOUT HIS SUPERVISOR GETTING ON HIS CASE ABOUT SELLING SHARES TO CLIENTS WHEN HE WAS WORKING IN THE CLINIC IN CINCINNATI. WHAT DID HE TELL YOU ABOUT ANYTHING SAID BY ANYONE IN BALD MOUNTAIN?

A   NOTHING. OH, FROM TIME TO TIME HE WOULD TALK ABOUT HIS CONTACTS WITH PROSPECTS AND HOW HE THOUGHT HE WAS GOING TO MAKE A SALE OR MAYBE NOT. BUT I DIDN'T HEAR ANYTHING ABOUT THE ATTITUDE OF REVEREND YUN, HIS SENIOR PASTOR, OR OTHER MEMBERS OF THE MINISTERIAL STAFF OR MEMBERS OF THE CHURCH COUNCIL. NOTHING.

Q   WERE YOU AWARE THAT HE WAS CONTINUING TO PROSPECT AMONG HIS COUNSELING CLIENTS AFTER HE ARRIVED IN BALD MOUNTAIN?

A   I ASSUMED HE WAS PROBABLY CONTINUING TO DO THAT, BUT I HAD

[Document page 15]

1   NOTHING TO CONFIRM IT.

2   Q   YOU TESTIFIED EARLIER THAT YOU BELIEVE YOU MAY HAVE MET PASTOR

3   YUN. CAN YOU BE MORE DEFINITE?

4   A   YES. REVISITING THESE TIMES HAS FLESHED OUT MY MEMORY.   I PAID A

5   FEW VISITS TO BALD MOUNTAIN IN YR-03 AND YR-02. JUST AS LINWOOD

6   VISITED CINCINNATI DURING SOME OF THE SAME PERIOD. I WOULD MEET HIM AT

7   HIS COUNSELING OFFICE AND WE WOULD GO OVER TO THE PARTNERSHIP OFFICE

8   AND CONDUCT WHATEVER BUSINESS WE HAD. I KNOW THAT THE FIRST TIME I

9   VISITED, LINWOOD GAVE ME A TOUR OF THE CHURCH, AND I REMEMBER AT THAT

10 TIME WE RAN INTO PASTOR YUN, AND HE INTRODUCED US. PASTOR YUN SAID

11 SOME VERY COMPLIMENTARY THINGS ABOUT LINWOOD, AND THAT WAS ABOUT IT.

12 THE NEXT TIME I CAME, LINWOOD SET UP A LITTLE LUNCH FOR ME WITH PASTOR

13 YUN AND A COUPLE OF THE ASSISTANT PASTORS.

14   Q   WHEN WAS THAT?

15   A   PROBABLY IN LATE YR-03 OR EARLY YR-02.

16   Q   WHICH ASSISTANT PASTORS?

17   A   I KNOW THAT ONE OF THEM WAS A PASTOR MARTIN, BUT I'M AFRAID I'VE

18 FORGOTTEN THE OTHER ONE'S NAME.

19   Q   WHAT DID THE FIVE OF YOU TALK ABOUT AT LUNCH?

20   A   OH, THE USUAL WHEN A BUNCH OF MINISTERS GET TOGETHER.   CHURCH

21 POLITICS. RAISING MONEY. PROGRAMS.   MAYBE SOMETIMES TALK ABOUT OUR

22 FAMILIES.

23   Q   WERE THE OTHERS CURIOUS ABOUT THE NATURE OF YOUR RELATIONSHIP

24 WITH LINWOOD?

25   A   NO. THEY KNEW I WAS AN OLD PAL AND COLLEAGUE FROM CINCINNATI AND

26 I SAID I HAD SOME BUSINESS IN MOBILE TO ATTEND TO AND HAD DROPPED BY

27 BALD MOUNTAIN ON THE WAY HOME.

[Document page 16]

Q   THAT WAS AN UNTRUTH?

A   YES. I WANTED TO DEFLECT INQUIRIES.

Q   DID ANYTHING COME UP DURING YOUR LUNCHEON CONVERSATION ABOUT LINWOOD'S COUNSELING PRACTICE?

A   NO, OTHER THAN HE SAID HE WAS WORKING HARD AND ENJOYING IT.

Q   DID ANY NAMES OF INDIVIDUALS ASSOCIATED WITH THE CHURCH COME UP?

A   NOT THAT I RECALL.

Q   DID ANYTHING COME UP ABOUT YOUR BED AND BREAKFAST ENTERPRISE WITH LINWOOD, YOUR LIMITED PARTNERSHIP, AND SUCH MATTERS?

A   NOT AT ALL.

Q   IT SEEMS STRANGE THAT THIS BUSINESS, WHICH WAS A VERY IMPORTANT PART OF YOUR LIFE AND THAT OF LINWOOD ROOKS, WOULD NOT EVEN BE MENTIONED.

A   THERE WERE CERTAIN VENUES WHERE WE FREELY DISCUSSED THE BUSINESS AND OTHERS WHERE WE DID NOT. BECAUSE OF THE CRITICISM THAT LINWOOD ENDURED IN CINCINNATI, WE AGREED TO STAY AWAY FROM THAT TOPIC.

Q   DO YOU HAVE ANY IDEA WHETHER REVEREND YUN OR ANYONE ELSE ASSOCIATED WITH BALD MOUNTAIN COMMUNITY CHURCH EVER HEARD ANYTHING ABOUT LINWOOD'S EFFORTS TO SELL SHARES TO HIS COUNSELING CLIENTS IN CINCINNATI OR ABOUT DR. NORTH'S INSTRUCTIONS THAT LINWOOD SHOULD STOP THAT ACTIVITY?

A   NO, I DO NOT.

Q   ANY OTHER CONTACTS WITH PASTOR YUN BESIDES THOSE TWO OCCASIONS?

A   I DON'T THINK SO.

Q   SO TO THE BEST OF YOUR KNOWLEDGE, REVEREND YUN HAD NO BASIS FOR KNOWING OR EVEN SUSPECTING THAT REVEREND ROOKS WAS SOLICITING HIS COUNSELING CLIENTS TO BUY SHARES IN THE BUSINESS OR EVEN DISCUSSING

[Document page 17]

1   THAT BUSINESS WITH HIS COUNSELING CLIENTS, AND TO THE BEST OF YOUR

2   KNOWLEDGE NO ONE ASSOCIATED WITH BALD MOUNTAIN COMMUNITY CHURCH HAD

3   ANY IDEA OR SUSPICION ALONG THOSE LINES?

4   MR. DUPRIEST:

5   I OBJECT TO THAT QUESTION AS COMPOUND, BUT IF THE WITNESS FEELS SHE

6   CAN HANDLE IT, I DON'T MIND.

7   THE WITNESS: I CAN HANDLE IT.   THE ANSWER IS NO.

8   MS. RUMSDALE:

9   THOSE ARE ALL MY QUESTIONS.

10   MR. DUPRIEST:

11   I DON'T HAVE ANY FOLLOW-UP, SO WE CAN DECLARE THIS DEPOSITION

12 CONCLUDED.

13   THE REPORTER:

14   USUAL STIPULATIONS, COUNSEL?

15   MR. DUPRIEST:

16   REVEREND BURR, WOULD YOU FEEL MORE COMFORTABLE IF YOU WERE ABLE TO

17 READ AND MAKE ANY CORRECTIONS IN THE TRANSCRIPT OF YOUR TESTIMONY

18 BEFORE MR. AHERN CERTIFIES THE TRANSCRIPT?

19   THE WITNESS:

20 WHAT'S THE USUAL PRACTICE?

21   MR. DUPRIEST:

22   WELL, MR. AHERN IS A DARN GOOD COURT REPORTER AND HIS TRANSCRIPTS

23 ARE VERY ACCURATE.   BOTH MS. RUMSDALE AND I WILL GET A CHANCE TO

24 REVIEW THE TRANSCRIPT AFTER IT IS CERTIFIED AND IF THERE'S ANY PROBLEM

25 WE CAN GET IN TOUCH WITH YOU AND MR. AHERN AND TAKE STEPS TO CORRECT

26 THE TRANSCRIPT. BUT IT'S YOUR CALL.

27   THE WITNESS:

1 LIFE IS TOO SHORT. I DON'T NEED TO REVIEW THE TRANSCRIPT IF BOTH OF

2 YOU ARE OK WITH THAT.

3 MR. DUPRIEST:

4 THANK YOU, MR AHERN. THE USUAL STIPULATIONS ARE FINE WITH ME.

5 MS. RUMSDALE:

6 SAME HERE.

7 (AT 11:35 A.M., MAY 24, YR-00, THE DEPOSITION OF HEATHER SEDALIA

8 BURR WAS ADJOURNED.)

9 //

10 //

11 //

12 //

13 //

14 //

15 //

16 //

17 //

18 //

19 //

20 //

21 //

22 //

23 //

24 //

25 //

26 //

27 //

1   <u>REPORTER'S CERTIFICATE</u>

2   I, LEONARD AHERN, OFFICIAL COURT REPORTER OF THE STATE OF ALABAMA,

3   HEREBY CERTIFY THAT THE FOREGOING DEPOSITION OF HEATHER SEDALIA BURR

4   WAS TAKEN BEFORE ME AT THE TIME AND PLACE HEREIN SET FORTH, AT WHICH

5   TIME THE WITNESS WAS PUT ON OATH BY ME;

6   THAT THE TESTIMONY OF THE WITNESS AND ALL OBJECTIONS MADE AT THE

7   TIME OF EXAMINATION WERE RECORDED STENOGRAPHICALLY BY ME, AND WERE

8   THEREAFTER TRANSCRIBED UNDER MY DIRECT SUPERVISION.

9   I FURTHER CERTIFY THAT I AM NEITHER COUNSEL FOR NOR RELATED TO ANY

10 PARTY TO SAID ACTION, NOR AM I IN ANYWISE INTERESTED IN THE OUTCOME

11 THEREOF.

12   IN WITNESS WHEREOF, I HAVE SUBSCRIBED MY NAME ON JUNE 3, YR-00.

                                        Leonard Ahern

IN THE UNITED STATES DISTRICT COURT
FOR THE WESTERN DISTRICT OF ALABAMA

ERNESTINE PETRILLO   :

    PLAINTIFF   :

                                 :

VS.   :   CIVIL ACTION NO. 00-85FD

                                 :

LINWOOD ROOKS, ET AL.   :

    DEFENDANTS   :

                                 :

UNITED STATES DISTRICT COURT
FILED
June 14, YR-00
WESTERN DISTRICT OF ALABAMA

DEPOSITION OF LELAND LAMPREY NORTH

TAKEN BY PLAINTIFF AT 900 MAPLE LANE, BALD MOUNTAIN, ALABAMA,
COMMENCING AT 7:00 A.M., MAY 31, YR-00, BEFORE LEONARD AHERN,
CERTIFIED STENOGRAPHIC REPORTER.

APPEARANCES:

    FOR PLAINTIFF:

        WILSON & DUPRIEST

            BY: ARMAND DUPRIEST, ESQ.

        900 MAPLE LANE
        BALD MOUNTAIN, ALABAMA 36918
        TELEPHONE (934) 333-2541

    FOR DEFENDANTS HARRIETT YUN AND BALD MOUNTAIN COMMUNITY CHURCH:

        MILLER, ELDRIDGE & PASTERNAK

            BY: EMILY RUMSDALE, ESQ.

        13304 BALD MOUNTAIN PARKWAY
        BALD MOUNTAIN, ALABAMA 36918
        TELEPHONE (934) 485-9000

1   BALD MOUNTAIN, ALABAMA, MAY 31, YR-00

2   LELAND LAMPREY NORTH

3   HAVING BEEN DULY SWORN, TESTIFIED AS FOLLOWS:

4   EXAMINATION ON BEHALF OF THE PLAINTIFF

5   MR. DUPRIEST:

6   DR. NORTH HAS TOLD ME THAT HE HAS LIMITED TIME FOR THIS DEPOSITION.

7   HE HAS A PLANE TO CATCH. HE CAME IN YESTERDAY ON UNRELATED BUSINESS

8   AND I THOUGHT WE MIGHT BE ABLE TO SQUEEZE A DEPOSITION IN AND AVOID

9   ALL OF US HAVING TO GO TO HIM IN CINCINNATI. HE GENEROUSLY AGREED TO

10 MEET US AT THIS EARLY HOUR IF WE WOULD PROMISE TO MAKE IT BRIEF.

11 THANK YOU DR. NORTH. WE APPRECIATE YOUR MAKING YOURSELF AVAILABLE ON

12 SUCH SHORT NOTICE. MR. AHERN IS ACQUAINTED WITH US AND I ASK HIM TO

13 NOTE OUR APPEARANCES. DR. NORTH HAS AN EXTENSIVE C.V. WHICH HE HAS

14 PROVIDED, AND I ASK THAT IT BE MARKED AS NORTH DEPOSITION EXHIBIT 1

15 AND BE ATTACHED TO THE TRANSCRIPT OF THIS DEPOSITION.

16   [NORTH DEPOSITION EXHIBIT 1 MARKED]

17 BY MR. DUPRIEST:

18   Q   YOU ARE LELAND LAMPREY NORTH.

19   A   YES.

20   Q   I UNDERSTAND THAT YOU HAVE GIVEN DEPOSITIONS MANY TIMES, THAT

21 YOU ARE AWARE OF THE PURPOSE OF DEPOSITIONS, YOU UNDERSTAND THE

22 PROTOCOL, YOU ARE AWARE OF THE OBLIGATION TO TELL THE TRUTH, AND YOU

23 HAVE TOLD ME YOU ARE IN GOOD HEALTH AND THERE IS NO REASON WHY YOU

24 CANNOT GIVE A DEPOSITION THIS MORNING. IS THAT CORRECT?

25   A   THAT'S CORRECT.

26   Q   I SHOW YOU NORTH DEPOSITION EXHIBIT 1,CONSISTING OF 35 PAGES. DO

27 YOU RECOGNIZE IT?

1   A THAT'S MY CURRICULUM VITA.

2   Q DOES IT FULLY AND ACCURATELY STATE ALL FACTS RELATING TO YOUR

3 EDUCATION, EMPLOYMENT, PROFESSIONAL LICENSURE, PROFESSIONAL SOCIETY

4 MEMBERSHIPS, PUBLICATIONS, AND ALL OTHER RELEVANT INFORMATION

5 CONCERNING YOUR PROFESSIONAL QUALIFICATIONS AND ATTAINMENTS?

6   A YES.

7   Q AMONG OTHER POSITIONS, YOU ARE CURRENTLY THE CLINICAL DIRECTOR

8 OF THE LEON LAMPREY NORTH COUNSELING CENTER IN CINCINNATI, AND YOU

9 HAVE HELD THAT POSITION FOR MANY YEARS?

10   A THAT IS CORRECT.

11   Q WOULD YOU HAPPEN TO KNOW WHY THE REVEREND HARRIETT YUN TESTIFIED

12 IN HER DEPOSITION THAT YOU WERE SITUATED IN NASHVILLE?

13   A I WAS ONCE AFFILIATED WITH A GRADUATE COUNSELING PROGRAM AT

14 VANDERBILT UNIVERSITY. PERHAPS THE REVEREND MS. YUN GOT IT MIXED UP.

15 BUT CINCINNATI IS CURRENTLY MY HOME AND WHERE I WORK.

16   Q IN CONNECTION WITH THAT WORK, YOU HAVE OCCASION TO SUPERVISE THE

17 CLINICAL WORK OF PERSONS WHO HAVE COMPLETED THEIR EDUCATION FOR A

18 CAREER IN COUNSELING AND NEED TO OBTAIN SUPERVISED PRACTICE EXPERIENCE

19 TO QUALIFY FOR UNCONDITIONAL LICENSURE?

20   A YES, BUT I SHOULD ADD THIS. MY INTERNS ARRIVE FROM VARIOUS

21 PATHWAYS. SOME ARE PSYCHIATRISTS, CLINICAL PSYCHOLOGISTS, MARRIAGE AND

22 FAMILY COUNSELORS, CLINICAL SOCIAL WORKERS, AND PASTORAL COUNSELORS.

23 ALL OF THE FIELDS THAT I HAVE MENTIONED HAVE LICENSURE REQUIREMENTS

24 EXCEPT PASTORAL COUNSELORS. I BELIEVE THAT SEPARATION OF CHURCH AND

25 STATE PRECLUDES STATE LICENSING OF CLERGY PEOPLE AS SUCH. HOWEVER, THE

26 VARIOUS ASSOCIATIONS OF PASTORAL COUNSELING HAVE THEIR CRITERIA FOR

27 MEMBERSHIP, WHICH COMMONLY INCLUDE SUPERVISED HOURS, AND I PAY

1   ATTENTION TO THE REQUIREMENTS OF THOSE ASSOCIATIONS.

2   Q   DO YOU KNOW LEONARD ROOKS?

3   A   I ASSUME YOU MEAN LINWOOD ROOKS.

4   Q   YES, I'M SORRY.

5   A   THE REVEREND MR. ROOKS WAS AN INTERN IN MY CLINIC FOR TWO YEARS,

6   FROM JULY YR-06 UNTIL JULY YR-04, AND THEREAFTER HE CONTINUED TO WORK

7   IN MY CLINIC AS A FULLY-QUALIFIED PASTORAL COUNSELOR UNTIL LATE JUNE

8   YR-03.

9   Q   DO YOU KNOW WHY MR. ROOKS LEFT YOUR CLINIC?

10   A   YES, IT WAS TO ANSWER A CALL FROM THE COMMUNITY CHURCH IN THIS

11 CITY FOR A MINISTER WHO COULD HEAD UP THE CHURCH'S PASTORAL COUNSELING

12 CENTER.

13   Q   DO YOU KNOW HOW MR. ROOKS FOUND OUT ABOUT THAT OPPORTUNITY?

14   A   YES.   I TOLD HIM ABOUT IT. MY OLD FRIEND AND COLLEAGUE THE

15 REVEREND HARRIETT YUN TELEPHONED ME AND SAID THAT SHE WAS LOOKING FOR

16 A FIRST-RATE PASTORAL COUNSELOR, ONE WHO WAS NOT TOO FAR ALONG IN HIS

17 CAREER SO THAT MONEY WOULD NOT BECOME AN ISSUE. I IMMEDIATELY THOUGHT

18 OF THE REVEREND MR. ROOKS, MENTIONED THE OPPORTUNITY TO HIM, AND HE

19 FOLLOWED UP.

20   Q   DID YOU DISCUSS REVEREND ROOKS' QUALIFICATIONS WITH REVEREND

21 YUN?

22   A   INFORMALLY, YES. I ASSUMED THAT SHE WOULD BE GETTING HIS RESUME

23 AND THAT THE FACTS ABOUT HIS EDUCATION, ORDINATION, AND EXPERIENCE AS

24 A COUNSELOR WOULD BE LISTED. I TALKED MORE IMPRESSIONISTICALLY.

25 LINWOOD IS AN EXCELLENT COUNSELOR. HE IS VERY GIFTED. HIS CLIENTS

26 TRUST HIM COMPLETELY. HIS COUNSELING SKILLS ARE FIRST RATE. THAT'S

27 WHAT I TOLD REVEREND YUN.

[Document page 4]

1   Q YOU HAD SOME TROUBLE WITH MR. ROOKS DURING THE TIME HE WORKED IN

2 YOUR CLINIC?

3   A WHAT DO YOU MEAN?

4   Q DIDN'T YOU FIND OUT THAT MR. ROOKS WAS TRYING TO SELL TO HIS

5 COUNSELING CLIENTS SHARES OF A BUSINESS ENTERPRISE THAT HE WAS

6 INVOLVED WITH?

7   A YES, THAT CAME TO MY ATTENTION. ONE OF THE COUNSELEES MENTIONED

8 IT. I TALKED WITH LINWOOD. I DON'T THINK HE FULLY APPRECIATED THE

9 ETHICAL DIMENSIONS OF WHAT HE WAS DOING. BUT THAT'S WHY COUNSELORS

10 HAVE SUPERVISED CLINICAL EXPERIENCE, SO THAT THEY CAN ENCOUNTER NEW

11 CHALLENGES AND LEARN FROM THEIR EXPERIENCE.

12   Q WHAT WAS THE NATURE OF THE BUSINESS ENTERPRISE HE WAS TRYING TO

13 PEDDLE?

14   A IT WAS A FASCINATING CONCEPT OF COMBINING REGULAR VACATIONS WITH

15 SPIRITUAL WORK. THAT KIND OF APPROACH HAS BEEN TRIED IN THE PAST, BUT

16 NOT WITH THE ELEGANCE THAT MR. ROOKS AND HIS PARTNER WERE PLANNING.

17   Q DID YOU REGARD IT AS WRONG OR PROFESSIONALLY INAPPROPRIATE FOR

18 MR. ROOKS TO BE PROMOTING HIS BUSINESS AMONG HIS CLIENTS?

19   A IT WAS CERTAINLY PROFESSIONALLY INAPPROPRIATE BECAUSE IT PUT MR.

20 ROOKS IN A POSITION OF CONFLICTING INTERESTS BETWEEN HIS CLIENTS AND

21 HIS BUSINESS. WRONG? I DON'T THINK SO. THIS WAS A VERY HIGH-MINDED

22 PROJECT THAT MR. ROOKS AND HIS PARTNER HAD COME UP WITH. I THINK HE

23 SINCERELY BELIEVED THAT THERE WERE CERTAIN PASTORAL COUNSELING CLIENTS

24 WHO WOULD BENEFIT BY BEING INVOLVED IN THE SPIRITUAL BED AND BREAKFAST

25 PROGRAM AT THE SAME TIME THEY WERE IN PASTORAL COUNSELING.

26   Q WHAT KINDS OF BENEFITS DID YOU FORESEE?

27   A WELL, I AM NOT SURE I KNEW ENOUGH ABOUT IT TO UNDERSTAND

1   PRECISELY THE NATURE OF THE BENEFITS AND HOW IT FIT IN WITH A

2   COUNSELING RELATIONSHIP. MY STATEMENT WAS ABOUT THE REVEREND MR.

3   ROOKS' SINCERITY AND BELIEFS, ABOUT WHICH I HAVE NO DOUBT.

4   Q   DID YOU INFORM YOURSELF ABOUT THE NATURE OF THE BUSINESS AND

5   ABOUT THE SALES PITCHES HE WAS MAKING TO HIS CLIENTS?

6   A   ONLY TO A LIMITED EXTENT. I LEARNED ABOUT THE GENERAL CONTOURS

7   OF THE BUSINESS. I DID NOT ASK HIM ABOUT SALES PITCHES. IT WAS CLEAR

8   TO ME THAT ANY KIND OF EFFORT TO SELL CLIENTS ON INVESTING IN HIS

9   BUSINESS SHOULD BE HALTED IMMEDIATELY.

10   Q   DID IT OCCUR TO YOU THAT DETAILS ABOUT THE NATURE OF THE

11 BUSINESS AND THE NATURE OF THE SALES EFFORTS MIGHT HAVE A BEARING ON

12 YOUR POTENTIAL LIABILITIES?

13   A   I AM SURE THAT OCCURRED TO ME, BUT I DID NOT HAVE TIME TO DO A

14 DETAILED INVESTIGATION. IT WAS A VERY SIMPLE MATTER. MR. ROOKS WAS

15 ENGAGING IN BEHAVIOR THAT PUT HIM IN A POSITION OF CONFLICTING

16 INTERESTS AND THAT BEHAVIOR HAD TO STOP.

17   Q   DID YOU CONFER WITH MR. ROOKS AFTER YOU HEARD ABOUT WHAT HE WAS

18 DOING?

19   A   OF COURSE. I TOLD HIM WHAT I HAD HEARD. HE CONFIRMED IT IN A

20 GENERAL WAY. I OUTLINED FOR HIM IN SOME DETAIL THE GENERALLY ACCEPTED

21 RISKS AND RULES INVOLVING CONFLICTING INTERESTS. I TOLD HIM IN NO

22 UNCERTAIN TERMS THAT THIS ACTIVITY HAD TO STOP FOR THE BENEFIT OF HIS

23 CLIENTS AND HIS OWN FUTURE CAREER. MR. ROOKS GAVE ME HIS WORD THAT HE

24 WOULD STOP, AND THAT WAS THE END OF THE MATTER.

25   Q   DID YOU EVER CHECK UP TO SEE WHETHER MR. ROOKS KEPT HIS PROMISE?

26   A   NO. I NEVER HAD ANY REASON TO THINK HE WOULD NOT. OUR

27 RELATIONSHIP WAS BASED ON TRUST. FURTHERMORE, I NEVER HEARD OF ANY

[Document page 6]

RECURRENCES.

Q   WOULD IT SURPRISE YOU TO KNOW THAT HIS BUSINESS PARTNER

TESTIFIED IN THESE VERY PROCEEDINGS THAT REVEREND ROOKS CONTINUED TO

SOLICIT HIS COUNSELING CLIENTS TO INVEST IN THIS BUSINESS VENTURE EVEN

AFTER YOU ADMONISHED HIM?

A   THAT WOULD BE VERY SURPRISING AND VERY DISAPPOINTING.

Q   WHAT COMMUNICATIONS DID YOU HAVE WITH REVEREND YUN WITH REGARD

TO REVEREND ROOKS' QUALIFICATIONS TO WORK IN HER CHURCH?

A   I BELIEVE THERE WERE THREE. THERE WAS HER INITIAL PHONE CALL IN

WHICH SHE ASKED IF I HAD ANY IDEAS FOR FILLING THIS POSITION AND I

RECOMMENDED THE REVEREND MR. ROOKS. THAT WAS AN EXTENDED CONVERSATION.

Q   WHEN WAS THAT?

A   IN MARCH OR MAYBE EARLY APRIL OF YR-03.

Q   WHAT WAS THE NEXT COMMUNICATION?

A   I DROPPED REVEREND YUN A LITTLE NOTE ACKNOWLEDGING THAT I HAD

RECEIVED HER INQUIRY AND STATING MY RECOMMENDATION OF THE REVEREND MR.

ROOKS. THIS WAS MORE OF A FORMALITY. I THOUGHT SHE MIGHT NEED

SOMETHING LIKE THAT TO SHOW TO THE CHURCH COUNCIL.

Q   WHEN WAS THE LAST TIME?

A   THAT WAS IN APRIL, AFTER MR. ROOKS HAD GONE TO BALD MOUNTAIN AND

HAD BEEN INTERVIEWED. PASTOR YUN TELEPHONED AND SAID SHE HAD SOME

QUESTIONS ABOUT MR. ROOKS THAT HAD COME UP IN THE COURSE OF THE

INTERVIEWS.

Q   WHAT SORT OF QUESTIONS?

A   I DON'T REMEMBER ALL OF THEM. I KNOW ONE QUESTION RELATED TO HIS

SEXUAL ORIENTATION, AND I REASSURED HER THERE WAS NO PROBLEM THERE.

LINWOOD HAS NEVER BEEN MARRIED, AND THAT MAY HAVE RAISED A RED FLAG.

1   SHE WANTED TO KNOW MORE ABOUT WHAT WE WERE PAYING HIM AND WHAT I

2   THOUGHT SHE WOULD HAVE TO OFFER HIM TO GET HIM TO ACCEPT. SHE TOLD ME

3   THAT IN ONE OF THE INTERVIEWS MR. ROOKS MADE A COMMENT THAT APPARENTLY

4   SOME OF THE INTERVIEWERS THOUGHT WAS RACIST. OTHERS THOUGHT IT WAS

5   NOT. WHEN I HEARD OF THE REMARK IT DID NOT SEEM RACIST AT ALL AND I

6   TOLD PASTOR YUN THAT. FURTHERMORE I TOLD HER THAT AS FAR AS I WAS

7   CONCERNED LINWOOD DID NOT HAVE A RACIST BONE IN HIS BODY.

8   Q   DID YOU TELL PASTOR YUN ABOUT MR. ROOKS' HISTORY OF SELLING

9   INVESTMENTS IN HIS COMPANY TO HIS CLIENTS?

10   A   NO. IT NEVER CAME UP.

11   Q   DON'T YOU THINK THAT WOULD BE RELEVANT INFORMATION FOR HER AND

12 HER CHURCH TO CONSIDER?

13   A   I DON'T KNOW. EACH ORGANIZATION NEEDS TO DECIDE FOR ITSELF WHAT

14 THE QUALIFICATIONS WILL BE AND TO ASK THEIR QUESTIONS ACCORDINGLY. THE

15 ONLY TIME I VOLUNTEER ANYTHING IN A REFERENCE CHECK IS WHEN I HAVE

16 GIVEN A POSITIVE RECOMMENDATION BUT THEN BECOME AWARE OF CONDUCT

17 INDICATING BAD CHARACTER. CONDUCT INDICATING BAD CHARACTER MAY OR NOT

18 BE TRUE AND ACCURATE. PEOPLE CAN LEARN FROM THEIR MISTAKES. BUT IF I

19 AM RECOMMENDING SOMEONE AND I AM AWARE OF ANYTHING THAT MIGHT

20 REASONABLY BE CONSTRUED AS CASTING ASPERSIONS ON THAT PERSON'S

21 CHARACTER, I WILL BRING IT UP.

22   Q   DIDN'T YOU THINK THAT MR. ROOKS' TRYING TO SELL SPECULATIVE

23 SECURITIES TO HIS COUNSELING CLIENTS, WHO GENERALLY ARE PEOPLE IN

24 VULNERABLE SITUATIONS, INDICATES SOMETHING ABOUT HIS CHARACTER?

25   A   YOUR QUESTION CONTAINS A NUMBER OF ASSUMPTIONS, AND I CAN

26 CERTAINLY IMAGINE A DIFFERENT SITUATION WHERE I MIGHT THINK THAT. IN

27 THIS CASE I WAS SATISFIED THAT THE REVEREND MR. ROOKS IS A PERSON OF

UNIMPEACHABLE CHARACTER AND THAT WHAT OCCURRED IN HIS WORK IN MY

CLINIC INDICATED A CERTAIN NAIVETE AND OBTUSENESS TO THE DETAILS OF

ETHICAL PRACTICE. I HAD EVERY REASON TO BELIEVE THAT THE REVEREND MR.

ROOKS HAD LEARNED FROM THIS EXPERIENCE. IT DID NOT OCCUR TO ME THAT I

SHOULD BRING IT UP ABSENT A QUESTION TO WHICH THE INFORMATION WOULD BE

A RELEVANT ANSWER.

Q   HOW MANY OTHER PEOPLE ASSOCIATED WITH THE BALD MOUNTAIN

COMMUNITY CHURCH WERE YOU IN COMMUNICATION WITH BEFORE AND DURING THE

TIME THAT MR. ROOKS WAS UNDER CONSIDERATION FOR THE PASTORAL

COUNSELING POSITION IN THAT CHURCH?

A   NO ONE.

Q   REALLY? DIDN'T ANY MEMBERS OF THE SEARCH COMMITTEE CONTACT YOU?

DIDN'T THE CHAIR WOMAN OF THE CHURCH COUNCIL, WHO WAS IN CHARGE OF THE

SEARCH, GET IN TOUCH WITH YOU?

A   NO.

Q   WAS THAT SURPRISING TO YOU?

A   IN OTHER CIRCUMSTANCES IT MIGHT BE. BUT PASTOR YUN IS A MOST

UNUSUAL PERSON. WHILE SHE HAS INSTALLED IN HER CHURCH THE FORMAL

MECHANISMS OF REPRESENTATIVE GOVERNANCE, EVERYONE KNOWS THAT SHE RUNS

THAT CHURCH. I ASSUME THAT MOST OF THE MEMBERS OF THE CHURCH COUNCIL

ARE AWARE OF HER INFLUENCE OVER CHURCH AFFAIRS AND THE COUNCIL'S VERY

LIMITED ROLE. I ASSUMED THAT IF PASTOR YUN WAS SATISFIED, THAT WAS

THE END OF THE MATTER.

THE WITNESS: MR. DUPRIEST, I HAVE ALMOST RUN OUT OF TIME IF I AM

GOING TO MAKE MY FLIGHT.

MR. DUPRIEST: I AM FINISHED. IF ANYTHING ELSE OCCURS TO ME, I WILL

ASK IT OF YOU IN A FORM THAT CAN BE ANSWERED IN WRITING FROM YOUR

1   OFFICE. MS. RUMSDALE?

2   MS. RUMSDALE: I HAVE NO QUESTIONS.

3   [THE WITNESS DEPARTS.]

4   THE REPORTER:

5   HAVE YOU MADE THE USUAL STIPULATIONS?

6   MR. DUPRIEST:

7   YES.

8   MS. RUMSDALE:

9   YES.

10   (AT 7:37 A.M., MAY 31, YR-00, THE DEPOSITION OF LELAND LAMPREY

11   NORTH WAS ADJOURNED.)

12   [EXHIBIT 1 ATTACHED TO THIS TRANSCRIPT IS OMITTED.]

13   //

14   //

15   //

16   //

17   //

18   //

19   //

20   //

21   //

22   //

23   //

REPORTER'S CERTIFICATE

I, LEONARD AHERN, OFFICIAL COURT REPORTER OF THE STATE OF ALABAMA, HEREBY CERTIFY THAT THE FOREGOING DEPOSITION OF LELAND LAMPREY NORTH WAS TAKEN BEFORE ME AT THE TIME AND PLACE HEREIN SET FORTH, AT WHICH TIME THE WITNESS WAS PUT ON OATH BY ME;

THAT THE TESTIMONY OF THE WITNESS AND ALL OBJECTIONS MADE AT THE TIME OF EXAMINATION WERE RECORDED STENOGRAPHICALLY BY ME, AND WERE THEREAFTER TRANSCRIBED UNDER MY DIRECT SUPERVISION.

I FURTHER CERTIFY THAT I AM NEITHER COUNSEL FOR NOR RELATED TO ANY PARTY TO SAID ACTION, NOR AM I IN ANYWISE INTERESTED IN THE OUTCOME THEREOF.

IN WITNESS WHEREOF, I HAVE SUBSCRIBED MY NAME ON JUNE 13, YR-00.

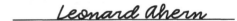

Leonard Ahern

IN THE UNITED STATES DISTRICT COURT
FOR THE WESTERN DISTRICT OF ALABAMA

```
                                      ┌─────────────────────────────────┐
                                      │  UNITED STATES DISTRICT COURT   │
                                      │             FILED               │
                                      │       June 14, YR-00            │
                                      │  WESTERN DISTRICT OF ALABAMA    │
                                      └─────────────────────────────────┘
```

ERNESTINE PETRILLO   :

     PLAINTIFF   :

VS.   :   CIVIL ACTION NO. 00-85FD

LINWOOD ROOKS, ET AL.   :

     DEFENDANTS   :

                              :

DEPOSITION OF LAURABELLE EPPERSON

TAKEN BY PLAINTIFF AT 900 MAPLE LANE, BALD MOUNTAIN, ALABAMA,
COMMENCING AT 10:15 A.M., JUNE 7, YR-00, BEFORE LEONARD AHERN,
CERTIFIED STENOGRAPHIC REPORTER.

APPEARANCES:

FOR PLAINTIFF:

     WILSON & DUPRIEST

         BY: ARMAND DUPRIEST, ESQ.

     900 MAPLE LANE
     BALD MOUNTAIN, ALABAMA 36918
     TELEPHONE (934) 333-2541

FOR DEFENDANTS HARRIETT YUN AND BALD MOUNTAIN COMMUNITY CHURCH:

     MILLER, ELDRIDGE & PASTERNAK

         BY: EMILY RUMSDALE, ESQ.

     13304 BALD MOUNTAIN PARKWAY
     BALD MOUNTAIN, ALABAMA 36918
     TELEPHONE   (934) 485-9000

BALD MOUNTAIN, ALABAMA, JUNE 7, YR-00

LAURABELLE EPPERSON

HAVING BEEN DULY SWORN, TESTIFIED AS FOLLOWS:

EXAMINATION ON BEHALF OF THE PLAINTIFF

MR. DUPRIEST:

THIS MORNING WE ARE TO TAKE THE DEPOSITION OF LAURABELLE EPPERSON IN THE CASE OF PETRILLO VS. ROOKS, ET AL, IN THE UNITED STATES DISTRICT COURT FOR THE WESTERN DISTRICT OF ALABAMA, NO. 00-85. MS. PETRILLO IS PRESENT. THE DEFENDANTS BALD MOUNTAIN COMMUNITY CHURCH AND HARRIETT YUN ARE REPRESENTED BY EMILY RUMSDALE, WHO IS PRESENT. I AM ARMAND DUPRIEST, THE ATTORNEY FOR THE PLAINTIFF, ERNESTINE PETRILLO. AND AS OUR COURT REPORTER TODAY WE ARE ONCE AGAIN BLESSED WITH THE EVER-WATCHFUL AND ALWAYS CHEERFUL LEONARD AHERN. IS IT A BIT HOT IN HERE? YES? I'LL HAVE THE THERMOSTAT TURNED DOWN.

[MR. DUPRIEST DEPARTS AND IMMEDIATELY RETURNS.]

MR. DUPRIEST:

GOOD MORNING, MS. EPPERSON.

THE WITNESS:

GOOD MORNING.

[PRELIMINARY QUESTIONS. SEE FOOTNOTE 4, PAGE 60, SUPRA.]

* * *

BY MR. DUPRIEST:

Q   MS. EPPERSON, WOULD YOU PLEASE TELL US A LITTLE BIT ABOUT YOURSELF. WHERE YOU'VE LIVED, YOUR FAMILY, YOUR EMPLOYMENT, AND YOUR AFFILIATION WITH THE BALD MOUNTAIN COMMUNITY CHURCH?

A   I AM ORIGINALLY FROM BESSEMER, BUT I HAVE LIVED IN BALD MOUNTAIN NEARLY ALL MY ADULT LIFE. MY HUSBAND IS FROM HERE AND WE DECIDED TO

1   SETTLE DOWN HERE IN BALD MOUNTAIN. MY HUSBAND WORKS AS AN ELECTRICIAN

2   AND I AM AN INDEPENDENT REAL ESTATE BROKER. WE HAVE THREE LOVELY

3   CHILDREN, AND I GUESS THAT IS ABOUT IT. OH YES, THE CHURCH. WE JOINED

4   THE BALD MOUNTAIN COMMUNITY CHURCH AROUND YR-16. THE WHOLE FAMILY

5   ATTENDS SERVICES AND SUNDAY SCHOOL ON A REGULAR BASIS. IN YR-08 I WAS

6   ELECTED TO THE CHURCH COUNCIL AND WAS REELECTED IN YR-06, YR-04, AND

7   YR-02. IN YR-04, ON REVEREND YUN'S NOMINATION, I WAS ELECTED CHAIR OF

8   THE CHURCH COUNCIL. I WAS REELECTED CHAIRPERSON IN YR-02.

9   Q   PLEASE DESCRIBE THE CHURCH COUNCIL.

10   A   THE COUNCIL CONSISTS OF 12 MEMBERS OF THE CHURCH WHO ARE ELECTED

11 TO STAGGERED TERMS OF TWO YEARS. THE COUNCIL IS THE GOVERNING BODY OF

12 THE CHURCH, SUBJECT, OF COURSE, TO THE ULTIMATE AUTHORITY OF THE

13 CONGREGATION ACTING IN A CONGREGATIONAL MEETING. WE HANDLE THE BUDGET.

14 WE APPOINT THE VARIOUS COMMITTEES THAT ARE NEEDED TO OPERATE THE

15 CHURCH PROGRAMS.

16   Q   WHAT IS THE RELATIONSHIP OF THE CHURCH COUNCIL TO THE PASTORAL

17 STAFF OF THE CHURCH?

18   A   WELL, TECHNICALLY, OUR PASTORS ARE ALL EMPLOYEES OF THE CHURCH.

19 THE CONGREGATION, UPON THE RECOMMENDATION OF THE CHURCH COUNCIL,

20 RECOMMENDS THE CREATION OR ABOLITION OF PASTORAL POSITIONS, AND IN

21 RECENT YEARS WE HAVE BEEN CLOSELY INVOLVED IN THE SELECTION OF PASTORS

22 FOR THE CHURCH. ALL OF THE PASTORS ARE HIRED AT WILL. THERE ARE NO

23 EMPLOYMENT CONTRACTS. WE OPERATE AT A VERY HIGH LEVEL OF TRUST. AND

24 THE CHURCH COUNCIL EXERCISES VERY LITTLE CONTROL OVER THE CONDUCT OF

25 THE PASTORS. THEY ARE CALLED BY GOD TO SERVE US, AND I GUESS WE

26 FIGURE THAT THE ALMIGHTY WILL SHOW OUR PASTORS WHAT NEEDS TO BE DONE.

27   Q   I UNDERSTAND THAT REVEREND HARRIETT YUN IS THE SENIOR PASTOR AND

THAT THERE ARE ABOUT A HALF DOZEN ASSOCIATE AND ASSISTANT PASTORS WHO FULFILL VARIOUS MINISTERIAL FUNCTIONS UNDER HER LEADERSHIP, RIGHT?

A   CORRECT.

Q   REVEREND YUN IS THE FOUNDING PASTOR OF THE CHURCH AND SHE REMAINS VERY INFLUENTIAL IN THE OVERALL POLICIES AND THE DAY TO DAY OPERATIONS OF THE CHURCH, YES?

A   OH, YES. REVEREND YUN IS AN EXTREMELY CHARISMATIC, EXTREMELY CAPABLE PERSON IN EVERYTHING SHE DOES. SHE DREW THE INITIAL CONGREGATION TO HERSELF AND LED THAT TINY CONGREGATION TO BECOME A VERY LARGE CONGREGATION OCCUPYING A MAGNIFICENT PHYSICAL PLANT. MOST PEOPLE WHO ATTEND OUR CHURCH COME TO HEAR REVEREND YUN. SHE IS AN INSPIRING PREACHER. AS THE FOUNDING PASTOR, REVEREND YUN DID EVERYTHING AT FIRST. WHY, SHE EVEN EMPTIED THE TRASH AND CLEANED THE BATHROOMS, I HAVE HEARD. AS THE CONGREGATION GREW AND THE COUNCIL AND COMMITTEES AROSE, SHE HAS BEEN ABLE TO DELEGATE THE MUNDANE RESPONSIBILITIES TO US AS WELL AS THE CUSTODIAL EMPLOYEES THAT WE HAVE ON OUR STAFF. I WOULD SAY THAT, WHILE WE HAVE THE FORMALITIES OF CONGREGATIONAL GOVERNANCE, NINETY FIVE PERCENT OF OUR IMPORTANT DECISIONS ARE ON THE RECOMMENDATION OF REVEREND YUN. SHE REMAINS A VISIONARY LEADER.

Q   HAS ANYTHING EVER COME UP WHERE THE CHURCH COUNCIL AND REVEREND YUN DISAGREED?

A   NOT REALLY. THREE YEARS AGO WE BEGAN A WEEKDAY DAY CARE CENTER. REVEREND YUN WAS OPPOSED TO THE IDEA. BUT WHEN SHE SAW HOW MUCH ENTHUSIASM THERE WAS, SHE CHANGED HER OPINION AND BECAME THE LEADER OF THE MOVEMENT TO GET THE DAY CARE CENTER FUNDED AND INTO APPROPRIATE FACILITIES. SHE DOES NOT THRIVE ON CONFLICT. SHE IS A CONSENSUS

1   BUILDER.

2   Q   HOW DOES THE CHURCH GO ABOUT HIRING PASTORS?

3   A   THE FIRST STEP IS THAT A POSITION NEEDS TO BE CREATED OR AN

4   EXISTING POSITION HAS BEEN VACATED. THE CONGREGATION VOTES ON WHETHER

5   TO SET UP A CALL COMMITTEE. THE CALL COMMITTEE IS RESPONSIBLE FOR

6   ADVERTISING THE VACANCY, SOLICITING APPLICATIONS, WEEDING THROUGH THE

7   APPLICATIONS TO FIND THE BEST ONES, AND THEN CONDUCTING BRIEF INITIAL

8   INTERVIEWS TO DECIDE WHOM TO INVITE FOR THE FULL BLOWN INTERVIEW

9   PROCESS.   WHILE THAT'S THE FORMAL PROCESS, YOU CAN BE SURE THAT

10 REVEREND YUN IS VERY CLOSELY INVOLVED.   THE LAST COUPLE OF TIMES THE

11 CONGREGATION HAS APPOINTED THE CHURCH COUNCIL TO SERVE AS THE CALL

12 COMMITTEE.

13   Q   WHAT WAS THE PROCESS BY WHICH LINWOOD ROOKS BECAME AN ASSOCIATE

14 PASTOR OF THE CHURCH AND HEAD OF THE PASTORAL COUNSELING CENTER?

15   A   THE PERSON THAT FILLED THAT POSITION LEFT UNDER RATHER

16 UNPLEASANT CIRCUMSTANCES IN JANUARY YR-03. IN ABOUT A MONTH, THE

17 CONGREGATION AUTHORIZED A SEARCH AND ASKED THE CHURCH COUNCIL TO SERVE

18 AS THE CALL COMMITTEE. I APPOINTED A SUBCOMMITTEE TO HANDLE THE

19 DETAILS OF THE SEARCH.   WE ADVERTISED THE POSITION AND HAD RECEIVED A

20 NUMBER OF APPLICATIONS WHEN REVEREND YUN PHONED ME AND SAID,

21 LAURABELLE I THINK I'VE FOUND THE MAN FOR THE COUNSELING POSITION. WE

22 CALLED A COUNCIL MEETING AND REVEREND YUN PRESENTED HIS CREDENTIALS

23 AND RECOMMENDATIONS, AND THE COUNCIL DECIDED RIGHT AWAY TO INVITE HIM

24 FOR AN INTERVIEW. HE WAS AT THE STAGE OF HIS CAREER WHEN OPPORTUNITIES

25 WOULD BE COMING HIS WAY THICK AND FAST, AND WE WANTED TO GET HIM

26 BEFORE SOME OTHER CHURCH BEAT US TO HIM. SO REVEREND ROOKS CAME TO

27 BALD MOUNTAIN IN MARCH AND WE INTERVIEWED HIM. SOME TIME LATER, WE

RECOMMENDED THAT THE CONGREGATION CALL HIM TO BE OUR NEXT ASSOCIATE

PASTOR IN CHARGE OF THE COUNSELING CENTER.

Q   DID YOU CHECK HIS REFERENCES?

A   FOR THE MOST PART WE RELIED ON REVEREND YUN FOR THAT. THERE'S A

VERY EMINENT COUNSELING TRAINER THAT REVEREND YUN KNOWS IN CINCINNATI.

SHE CHECKED WITH HIM AND GOT GLOWING RECOMMENDATIONS FOR REVEREND

ROOKS.

Q   DO YOU KNOW THAT PERSON'S NAME?

A   YES, IT WAS A DR. NORTH, LELAND LAMPREY NORTH.   REVEREND YUN

TOLD US THAT HE WAS THE VERY TOPS IN THE FIELD AND ANY PASTORAL

COUNSELOR WHO HAD TRAINED UNDER HIM WOULD BE HIGHLY QUALIFIED.

Q   ARE YOU SAYING THAT NEITHER YOU NOR ANY OTHER MEMBER OF THE

CHURCH COUNCIL COMMUNICATED WITH THIS DR. NORTH?

A   THAT'S RIGHT.

Q   AND THAT NEITHER YOU OR ANY OTHER MEMBER OF THE CHURCH COUNCIL

VERIFIED THE CLAIMS MADE ON REVEREND ROOKS' C.V. OR COMMUNICATED WITH

HIS PREVIOUS EMPLOYERS, PROFESSORS, AND THE LIKE, THE PEOPLE HE LISTED

AS REFERENCES?

A   WE DID NOT THINK THAT WAS NECESSARY. FRANKLY, I DON'T THINK WE

WERE INTERESTED IN WHAT SOME FORMER PROFESSORS MIGHT SAY. WE WERE

CONSIDERING HIM FOR A POSITION INVOLVING AN ACTIVE COUNSELING

PRACTICE.   HE HAD DONE ALL OF HIS CLINICAL WORK TO BECOME QUALIFIED AS

A PASTORAL COUNSELOR UNDER DR. NORTH.

Q   PRIOR TO THAT, HADN'T HE DONE GRADUATE WORK IN PASTORAL

COUNSELING AND RECEIVED AN ADVANCED DEGREE?

A   I BELIEVE SO.

Q   BUT YOU DIDN'T CHECK WITH ANYONE AT THE DIVINITY SCHOOL WHERE HE

1   HAD EARNED THAT DEGREE?

2   A   WE DID NOT THINK IT WAS NECESSARY. ACADEMIC ACHIEVEMENT IS OF

3   LIMITED VALUE IN EVALUATING A PERSON FOR A CLINICAL POSITION.

4   Q   WHEN YOU FIRST STARTED THE SEARCH PROCESS IN EARLY YR-03, WAS

5   ANY EFFORT MADE TO AGREE ON THE CRITERIA AND QUALIFICATIONS YOU WERE

6   LOOKING FOR?

7   A   OH, DEFINITELY. THE COUNCIL AND REVEREND YUN WENT ON A TWO DAY

8   RETREAT IN WHICH WE SHARED OUR THOUGHTS AND FEELINGS AND PRAYED A LOT

9   IN COMING UP WITH A PORTRAIT OF OUR IDEAL ASSOCIATE PASTOR FOR

10 COUNSELING. I THINK WE CAME AWAY WITH A CONSENSUS.

11   Q   CAN YOU DESCRIBE THAT CONSENSUS?

12   A   WELL, APART FROM EXCELLENT TRAINING AND CLINICAL EXPERIENCE, I

13 THINK WE WANTED SOMEONE WHO WAS MATURE, HAD GOOD BOUNDARIES, AND COULD

14 BE TRUSTED TO MAINTAIN CONFIDENTIALITY. WE WERE ALSO CONCERNED THAT

15 THE PERSON'S IDEAS ABOUT THE RELATIONSHIP BETWEEN COUNSELING AND

16 RELIGION WAS COMPATIBLE WITH OUR CHURCH. AND WE WERE ESPECIALLY

17 SENSITIVE TO ANY HINT OF SEXUAL IMPROPRIETY, SINCE THAT HAD BEEN AN

18 ISSUE WITH THE PREVIOUS OCCUPANT OF THAT POSITION.

19   Q   HOW DID YOU SATISFY YOURSELVES THAT REVEREND ROOKS FIT THAT

20 DESCRIPTION?

21   A   REVEREND YUN GAVE US A COMPLETE RUN-DOWN ON HER CONVERSATION

22 WITH DR. NORTH. THEY HAD AN EXTENDED CONVERSATION AND IT COVERED ALL

23 THE BASES. REVEREND ROOKS GOT A'S IN EVERY CATEGORY.

24   Q   DID REVEREND YUN REPORT ANY NEGATIVES?

25   A   NONE WHATSOEVER.

26   Q   DID SHE ASK DR. NORTH ABOUT WHETHER MR. ROOKS HAD ENGAGED IN ANY

27 INAPPROPRIATE CONDUCT WHILE SERVING IN HIS CLINICAL TRAINING PROGRAM?

A   WELL I KNOW SHE COVERED THE ISSUE OF SEXUAL BOUNDARIES. IN FACT SHE EVEN HAD A SECOND CONVERSATION WITH DR. NORTH WHEN ONE OR TWO OF THE COUNCIL MEMBERS HAD QUESTIONS ABOUT REVEREND ROOKS' SEXUAL ORIENTATION. OTHER THAN THAT, I DON'T KNOW.

Q   ARE YOU AWARE OF THE FACT THAT WHILE HE WAS WORKING IN DR. NORTH'S CLINICAL TRAINING PROGRAM, MR. ROOKS WAS REPRIMANDED FOR PLACING HIMSELF IN A CONFLICT OF INTEREST SITUATION INVOLVING HIS CLIENTS?

A   NO. THAT NEVER CAME UP.

Q   DO YOU KNOW WHETHER REVEREND YUN ASKED THE KIND OF QUESTIONS THAT WOULD HAVE DUG THAT OUT?

A   NOT REALLY. WE TRUSTED HER IMPLICITLY TO FIND OUT ALL RELEVANT INFORMATION.

Q   HAD YOU KNOWN OF REVEREND ROOKS' EFFORTS TO GET HIS CLIENTS IN COUNSELING TO INVEST IN HIS OUTSIDE BUSINESS ENTERPRISE, DO YOU THINK THE COUNCIL WOULD HAVE RECOMMENDED REVEREND ROOKS TO THE CONGREGATION?

A   I AM SURE IT WOULD HAVE GIVEN US PAUSE. BUT I CAN'T SAY FOR CERTAIN. I WOULD HAVE TO KNOW MORE ABOUT IT. HE WAS AT THAT STAGE AN APPRENTICE, AND APPRENTICES ARE EXPECTED TO MAKE MISTAKES. THAT'S HOW THEY LEARN AND GROW. I WOULD HAVE TO KNOW MORE.

Q   DID ANYONE ON THE CHURCH COUNCIL OR ANYONE IN THE CONGREGATION MAKE ANY INDEPENDENT INQUIRIES INTO REVEREND ROOKS' QUALIFICATIONS, WORK HISTORY, OR ANYTHING ELSE THAT WOULD BE RELEVANT TO DETERMINING HIS FITNESS FOR THIS POSITION?

A   NOT TO MY KNOWLEDGE. YOU HAVE TO UNDERSTAND THAT REVEREND YUN HAD DISCOVERED HIM AND WAS BASICALLY SPONSORING HIM. IN THAT SITUATION, WE WOULD RELY ENTIRELY ON REVEREND YUN AND FOLLOW HER

1   RECOMMENDATIONS.

2   Q   AFTER REVEREND ROOKS ACCEPTED THE CALL AND BEGAN HIS MINISTRY AT

3   BALD MOUNTAIN COMMUNITY CHURCH, DID THE CHURCH COUNCIL DO ANYTHING TO

4   EVALUATE HIS PERFORMANCE?

5   A   NOT REALLY.

6   Q   DID YOU HEAR FROM MEMBERS OF THE CONGREGATION ABOUT HOW HE WAS

7   DOING?

8   A   NOT IN ANY OFFICIAL WAY. BUT I DID HEAR FROM A NUMBER OF CHURCH

9   MEMBERS HOW MUCH THEY LIKED REVEREND ROOKS AND HOW HE SEEMED TO HAVE

10   BREATHED NEW LIFE INTO THE COUNSELING CENTER. ALSO, MANY PEOPLE

11   COMMENTED THAT HE WAS A VERY GOOD PREACHER, A TALENT TO WHICH OUR

12   CONGREGATION ATTACHES GREAT IMPORTANCE.

13   Q   WHEN DID REVEREND ROOKS' ACTIVITIES WITH REGARD TO PROMOTING AND

14   SELLING INTERESTS IN THE LIMITED PARTNERSHIP THAT WAS SET UP TO DO

15   THIS BED AND BREAKFAST BUSINESS, WHEN DID THAT FIRST COME TO YOUR

16   ATTENTION?

17   A   REVEREND YUN REPORTED TO US IN MAY YR-01 THAT REVEREND ROOKS HAD

18   REQUESTED AND SHE HAD GRANTED HIM A LEAVE OF ABSENCE. SHE DID NOT AT

19   THAT TIME GIVE US MANY DETAILS. IN JULY SHE TOLD US THAT HE HAD

20   RESIGNED, AND SHE GAVE US A BASIC RUN DOWN ON WHAT HAD HAPPENED. AND

21   OF COURSE IN JANUARY OF THIS YEAR, WHEN MS. PETRILLO BROUGHT HER LAW

22   SUIT, WE QUESTIONED REVEREND YUN VERY CLOSELY ABOUT WHAT HAD HAPPENED.

23   Q   AT THAT POINT THE HORSE HAD ALREADY LEFT THE BARN.

24   A   THAT'S RIGHT. BUT WE HAD TO HIRE COUNSEL TO REPRESENT US AND

25   TRY TO DETERMINE WHAT THE CHURCH'S EXPOSURE MIGHT BE.

26   Q   WASN'T COUNSEL PROVIDED BY THE CHURCH'S LIABILITY INSURANCE

27   CARRIER?

[Document page 9]

A   THE INSURANCE COMPANY DENIED COVERAGE AND WE WERE ON OUR OWN.

MR. DUPRIEST:

I DON'T HAVE ANY MORE QUESTIONS AT THIS TIME. MS. RUMSDALE, DID YOU WANT TO QUESTION THE WITNESS?

MS. RUMSDALE:

YES, THANK YOU.

EXAMINATION ON BEHALF OF THE DEFENDANTS

BY MS. RUMSDALE:

Q   MS. EPPERSON, YOU TESTIFIED THAT THE CHURCH COUNCIL WAS CONCERNED ABOUT APPLICANTS' IDEAS AS TO THE RELATIONSHIP BETWEEN COUNSELING AND RELIGION. WHAT IDEAS WERE YOU LOOKING FOR?

A   LET ME ANSWER YOU THIS WAY. THERE ARE TWO EXTREMES IN THE PRACTICE OF PASTORAL COUNSELING. ON ONE END ARE COUNSELORS WHO CONDUCT COUNSELING AS IF IT WAS A BIBLE STUDY CLASS, AND SPEND MOST OF THE TIME WITH CLIENTS OFFERING BIBLICAL COMMENTARIES ON THE THINGS GOING ON IN THEIR LIVES. THEY MAY USE BIBLE PASSAGES TO COMFORT THEIR CLIENTS. THEY MAY USE OTHER PASSAGES TO ENCOURAGE THEIR CLIENTS TO STOP CERTAIN TYPES OF DESTRUCTIVE OR SINFUL BEHAVIOR. AT THE OTHER EXTREME ARE PASTORAL COUNSELORS WHO ARE INDISTINGUISHABLE FROM SECULAR CLINICAL PSYCHOLOGISTS OR MARRIAGE COUNSELORS. WE DIDN'T WANT THAT EITHER. PEOPLE PICK PASTORAL COUNSELING OVER OTHER FORMS OF COUNSELING BECAUSE THEY BELIEVE THEY ARE HAVING A SPIRITUAL CRISIS ALONG WITH EVERYTHING ELSE, AND WE WANTED ANYONE WE HIRED TO BE SENSITIVE TO THE SPIRITUAL DIMENSION OF THEIR CLIENTS' NEEDS. FOR ANOTHER THING, OUR CHURCH IS VERY LIBERAL ON THE MATTER OF INTERPRETING THE BIBLE. WE ARE NOT PART OF A LARGER DENOMINATION WITH OFFICIAL STATEMENTS OF BELIEFS AND CREEDS TO WHICH WE MUST SUBSCRIBE. WE AVOID DOGMA AND ORTHODOXY AS

1 MUCH AS POSSIBLE. ACCORDING TO REVEREND YUN, THE BIBLE IS THE

2 INSPIRED WORD OF GOD DELIVERED TO MANKIND FOR MANKIND'S REDEMPTION. IT

3 IS NOT DELIVERED THROUGH INTERMEDIARIES BUT DIRECTLY TO EACH OF US.

4 ACCORDING TO REVEREND YUN, YOU OR I OR ANYONE ELSE IS EQUALLY

5 COMPETENT TO READ AND UNDERSTAND THE BIBLE. WHEN SHE PREACHES ON

6 BIBLICAL TEXTS, SHE OFTEN WILL COMMENT ABOUT HOW HER INTERPRETATION IS

7 NOT THE ONLY POSSIBLE ONE. SO IT WAS A MIDDLE GROUND BETWEEN SUPER

8 RELIGIOSITY AND TOTAL SECULARISM WE WERE LOOKING FOR, AND WE WERE

9 ESPECIALLY LOOKING FOR AN INDIVIDUAL WHO DID NOT HOLD DOCTRINAIRE

10 RELIGIOUS BELIEFS.

11   Q   WHAT DID YOU DO TO INSURE YOURSELVES THAT REVEREND ROOKS MET

12 THESE QUALIFICATIONS?

13   A   REVEREND YUN'S INTERVIEW WITH DR. NORTH COVERED THAT. I

14 UNDERSTAND THAT DR. NORTH IS NOT A PASTORAL COUNSELOR AS SUCH, BUT HE

15 IS VERY FAMILIAR WITH PASTORAL COUNSELING. AND I AM SURE THAT REVEREND

16 YUN AND DR. NORTH COVERED THE SUBJECT OF MR. ROOKS' POSITION REGARDING

17 THE ROLE OF RELIGION AND RELIGIOUS TEXTS IN PASTORAL COUNSELING.

18   Q   YOU SAY YOU ARE SURE. DID REVEREND YUN SAY THAT?

19   A   NOT IN SO MANY WORDS, BUT SHE IS VERY SENSITIVE TO THESE

20 CONCERNS THAT I CANNOT BELIEVE SHE WOULD HAVE SKIPPED OVER THIS. IN

21 ANY EVENT, REVEREND ROOKS CAME DOWN TO BALD MOUNTAIN FOR A DAY OR A

22 DAY AND A HALF OF INTERVIEWING WITH REPRESENTATIVE MEMBERS OF THE

23 CHURCH AND THE PASTORS. YOU CAN BE SURE THAT THIS WAS A PRIME TOPIC.

24   Q   COULD A WELL-RECOMMENDED PASTORAL COUNSELOR WHOM YOU DISCOVERED

25 TO HAVE DOCTRINAIRE BELIEFS ON SOMETHING LIKE, SAY, HOMOSEXUALITY –

26 COULD SUCH A PERSON HAVE BEEN CHOSEN FOR THIS JOB?

27   A   I WOULD SAY NO. THERE ARE DIVERSE VIEWS IN THE CONGREGATION

ABOUT THE BIBLE'S POSITION ON HOMOSEXUALITY, BUT NO ONE WANTS TO FORCE THEIR VIEWS ON ANYONE ELSE. WELL, I SHOULDN'T SAY NO ONE WANTS TO, BUT JUST THAT THE PREVAILING SPIRIT OF OUR CONGREGATION WELCOMES A DIVERSITY OF VIEWS AND NO EFFORT IS MADE TO CONVERT PEOPLE FROM ONE SIDE TO THE OTHER ON RELIGIOUS QUESTIONS. A SO-CALLED PASTORAL COUNSELOR WHO DID NOT SHARE THAT ATTITUDE WOULD HAVE A VERY DIFFICULT TIME FITTING IN WITH THE OTHER PASTORS AND THE CONGREGATION.

Q   AS A MATTER OF FACT, SOME CONCERN CAME UP ABOUT REVEREND ROOKS' SEXUAL ORIENTATION DIDN'T IT?

A   THERE ARE ONE OR TWO PEOPLE ON THE COUNCIL WHO THINK THAT A GROWN MAN WHO IS NOT MARRIED MUST BE GAY. THAT'S SILLY. BUT THEY INSISTED THAT WE CHECK IT OUT, AND WE DID.

Q   HOW DID YOU GO ABOUT CHECKING IT OUT?

A   REVEREND YUN GOT IN TOUCH WITH DR. NORTH, RAISED THE QUESTION, AND REPORTED BACK TO US. SHE SAID THERE WAS NO PROBLEM IN THIS AREA AND SHE REITERATED HER STRONG SUPPORT FOR REVEREND ROOKS' CANDIDACY.

Q   WOULD A GAY PERSON BE DISQUALIFIED FROM BEING YOUR CHURCH'S ASSOCIATE PASTOR FOR COUNSELING?

A   I DON'T THINK SO. BUT I CAN'T SPEAK FOR EVERYONE. ONE OF OUR ASSISTANT PASTORS IS GAY. HE IS ALSO CELIBATE. HE IS VERY WELL LIKED IN THE CONGREGATION AND HIS SEXUAL ORIENTATION IS NOT AN ISSUE. THERE MAY BE DIFFERENT CONSIDERATIONS FOR A PASTORAL COUNSELOR, BUT WE NEVER HAD TO GET INTO THEM IN THIS CASE.

Q   WAS IT UNUSUAL FOR THE CHURCH COUNCIL TO RELY SO HEAVILY ON REVEREND YUN IN THIS SEARCH AND HIRING PROCESS?

A   NOT AT ALL. IT IS THE NORM AT OUR CHURCH. REVEREND YUN IS A STRONG LEADER IN WHOM WE HAVE ENORMOUS TRUST.

[Document page 12]

1   MS. RUMSDALE:

2   THANK YOU, MS. EPPERSON. I HAVE NO FURTHER QUESTIONS.

3   MR. DUPRIEST:

4   OK, I GUESS WE CAN ADJOURN. THE USUAL STIPULATIONS, MR. AHERN.

5   THE REPORTER:

6   IS THAT AGREEABLE, MS. RUMSDALE?

7   MS. RUMSDALE:

8   YES.

9   (AT 11:00 A.M., JUNE 7, YR-00, THE DEPOSITION OF LAURABELLE

10 EPPERSON WAS ADJOURNED.)

11 //

12 //

13 //

14 //

15 //

16 //

17 //

18 //

19 //

20 //

21 //

22 //

23 //

24 //

25 //

26 //

27 //

<u>REPORTER'S CERTIFICATE</u>

I, LEONARD AHERN, OFFICIAL COURT REPORTER OF THE STATE OF ALABAMA, HEREBY CERTIFY THAT THE FOREGOING DEPOSITION OF LAURABELLE EPPERSON WAS TAKEN BEFORE ME AT THE TIME AND PLACE HEREIN SET FORTH, AT WHICH TIME THE WITNESS WAS PUT ON OATH BY ME;

THAT THE TESTIMONY OF THE WITNESS AND ALL OBJECTIONS MADE AT THE TIME OF EXAMINATION WERE RECORDED STENOGRAPHICALLY BY ME, AND WERE THEREAFTER TRANSCRIBED UNDER MY DIRECT SUPERVISION.

I FURTHER CERTIFY THAT I AM NEITHER COUNSEL FOR NOR RELATED TO ANY PARTY TO SAID ACTION, NOR AM I IN ANYWISE INTERESTED IN THE OUTCOME THEREOF.

IN WITNESS WHEREOF, I HAVE SUBSCRIBED MY NAME ON JUNE 12, YR-00.

Leonard Ahern

In the
United States District Court
for the Western District of Alabama

UNITED STATES DISTRICT COURT
FILED
July 7, YR-00
WESTERN DISTRICT OF ALABAMA

Ernestine Petrillo,	)	
	)	
Plaintiff	)	Civil Action No. 00-85FD
v.	)	
	)	
Linwood Rooks, et al.	)	
	)	
Defendants	)	

DEFAULT JUDGMENT

[This document is important for telling the story of *Petrillo v. Rooks* completely. However, the document itself is omitted because it is not important to the merits of the claims against BMCC and Rev. Yun.

[Plaintiff is entitled to a default judgment against Rev. Rooks because of his failure to appear and defend the action. Fed. R. Civ. P. 55 sets forth a three-step procedure for securing a default judgment. First, once the time for answering or otherwise responding to the complaint has expired, the plaintiff[5] may prove that fact by affidavit to the clerk of the court, and the clerk "shall enter" the default. This is a ministerial notation. Second, once the default has been entered, the plaintiff may make a motion for a default judgment. The

---

[5]A defendant who has filed a counterclaim or cross-claim against another party may also use the default judgment procedure. However, for simplicity, we refer to a plaintiff securing a default judgment against a defendant, as in the instant case.

[Document page 1]

motion should be accompanied by proof of the damages sought. Where plaintiff's claim "is for a sum certain or for a sum which can by computation be made certain," the clerk of the court is authorized to take the third step and enter a formal default judgment against the defendant. Fed. R. Civ. P. 55(b)(1). This judgment may be executed by seizing the defendant's property, garnishing wages, and the like. It may be sued upon in foreign jurisdictions. In all other cases the motion for a default judgment goes before a judge, who takes whatever steps may be necessary to ascertain the damages. Fed. R. Civ. P. 55(b)(2). This may include an evidentiary hearing. When the damages have been ascertained, they will be incorporated in a formal default judgment.

[If the defendant has no property, why would the plaintiff bother with a default judgment? There are two reasons. First, a default judgment may be executed against after-acquired property. Rev. Rooks may not remain penniless forever. Second, in an action involving more than one defendant, where at least one of those defendants appears and defends, default judgments against the others help clear the decks for an eventual appeal of the decision involving the active defendants. Generally speaking, appeals may be taken only from "final judgments" of district courts, *i.e.*, those that dispose of all claims as to all parties. 28 U.S.C. § 1291. If the action against Rev. Rooks was not wound up before the claims against BMCC and Yun are decided, the judgment as to BMCC and Rev. Yun would not be regarded as a final judgment. While there are mechanisms for overcoming this hurdle, see Fed. R. Civ. P. 54(b), the default judgment is an effective course.

[The rules for setting aside default judgments are contained in Fed. R. Civ. P. 55(c) and 60(b).]

Emily Rumsdale
Miller, Eldridge & Pasternak
13304 Bald Mountain Parkway
Bald Mountain, Alabama 36918
Telephone (934) 485-9000

UNITED STATES DISTRICT COURT
FILED
August 10, YR-00
WESTERN DISTRICT OF ALABAMA

Attorney for Defendants
Rev. Harriett Yun and
Bald Mountain Community Church

In the
United States District Court
for the Western District of Alabama

Ernestine Petrillo,	)	
	)	
Plaintiff	)	
	)	
v.	)	Civil Action No. 00-85FD
	)	
Linwood Rooks, et al.	)	
	)	
Defendants	)	

DEFENDANTS' MOTION FOR SUMMARY JUDGMENT

The defendants Bald Mountain Community Church ("BMCC") and Rev. Harriett Yun ("Yun") hereby move the court for a summary judgment dismissing with prejudice all claims asserted against them in the Complaint, on the grounds that all the papers on file in this case establish that there is no genuine issue as to any material fact, and that the defendants are entitled to judgment as a matter of law. This motion is brought pursuant to Fed. R. Civ. P. 56(b).

[Document page 1]

The only claims asserted against these defendants are in Counts Four, Five, and Six of the Complaint.

1. As to Count Four, all the papers on file in this case establish without dispute that:

    a)   the defendant Rooks was not a servant or employee of either the defendant BMCC or the defendant Yun, but rather, he was an independent contractor, because neither BMCC nor Yun controlled or had the right to control his conduct as Associate Pastor of BMCC and Director of BMCC's Pastoral Counseling Center; and

    b) If the defendant Rooks was a servant or employee of either the defendant BMCC or the defendant Yun, he was not acting within the scope of his employment when he engaged in the conduct alleged against him in the complaint.

2. As to both Counts Five and Six:

    a)   There is a complete absence of admissible evidence showing that either BMCC or Yun was negligent in either hiring or supervising the defendant Rooks.

    b) Adjudication of those claims and any relief with respect to those claims would violate the First Amendment of the United States Constitution.

c) Adjudication of those claims and any relief with respect to those claims would violate Amendment No. 622 to the Alabama Constitution, the Alabama Religious Freedom Amendment.

The relevant evidence in this case is contained in the depositions of Harriett Yun (filed April 2, YR-00), Ernestine Petrillo (filed April 14, YR-00), Linwood Rooks (filed June 3, YR-00), Heather Sedalia Burr (filed June 4, YR-00), Leland Lamprey North (filed June 14, YR-00), and Laurabelle Epperson (filed June 14, YR-00).

For the reasons stated herein and more fully developed in the Memorandum accompanying this motion, the defendants request a summary judgment dismissing with prejudice all claims against them in the Complaint.

Dated: August 9, YR-00

Respectfully submitted,

Emily Rumsdale

Emily Rumsdale
Miller, Eldridge & Pasternak
13304 Bald Mountain Parkway
Bald Mountain, Alabama 36918
Telephone (934) 485-9000

Attorney for Defendants
Rev. Harriett Yun and
Bald Mountain Community Church

CERTIFICATE OF SERVICE

I certify that on this 9th day of August, YR-00, I served the foregoing Defendants' Motion for Summary Judgment upon the plaintiff by causing a copy thereof to be hand-delivered to the attorney for the plaintiff, Armand DuPriest, at Wilson & DuPriest, 900 Maple Lane, Bald Mountain, Alabama 36918.

Emily Rumsdale
_____

Emily Rumsdale
Miller, Eldridge & Pasternak
13304 Bald Mountain Parkway
Bald Mountain, Alabama 36918
Telephone (934) 485-9000

Attorney for Defendants
Rev. Harriett Yun and
Bald Mountain Community Church